MW01119544

Criminal Justice
Recent Scholarship

Edited by
Nicholas P. Lovrich

A Series from LFB Scholarly

Youth Involvement in Crime
The Importance of Locus of Control and Collective Efficacy

Eileen M. Ahlin

LFB Scholarly Publishing LLC
El Paso 2013

Library of Congress Cataloging-in-Publication Data

Ahlin, Eileen.
  Youth involvement in crime : the importance of locus of control and collective efficacy / Eileen M. Ahlin.
     p. cm.
  Includes bibliographical references and index.
  ISBN 978-1-59332-526-8 (hardcover : alk. paper)
  1. Juvenile delinquency--Illinois--Chicago. 2. Locus of control--Illinois--Chicago. 3. Neighborhoods--Illinois--Chicago. 4. Social control--Illinois--Chicago. 5. Juvenile delinquency. 6. Locus of control. I. Title.
  HV9106.C4A36 2013
  364.3609773'11--dc23
                                    2012040464

ISBN 978-1-59332-526-8

Printed on acid-free 250-year-life paper.

Manufactured in the United States of America.

Table of Contents

List of Tables

List of Figures

Preface

The concepts of locus of control and collective efficacy have been used by scholars to explain involvement in individual-level crime. Scholars have found that both locus of control and collective efficacy are related to crime at the individual-level. However, research examining the relationship between locus of control and collective efficacy and its influence on youths' involvement in crime is scant. This study uses the Project on Human Development in Chicago Neighborhoods (PHDCN) data to examine the independent influences of locus of control and collective efficacy on involvement in crime among youths ages 9 to 19, and to also explore the potential moderating effect of collective efficacy on the relationship between locus of control and crime.

The relationship between locus of control, collective efficacy, and crime is addressed by asking three questions. First, does a youth's locus of control orientation influence their involvement in crime? Second, does collective efficacy influence youths' involvement in crime? Third, does collective efficacy moderate the relationship between locus of control and crime? Neighborhood context, family context, and individual-level demographic variables are also examined to control for the contexts in which youths live and individual factors that can influence involvement in crime.

Using hierarchical linear modeling, the analyses indicate mixed support for a relationship between locus of control, collective efficacy, and crime. A significant negative relationship exists between an internal locus of control and crime however no significant effects emerge between collective efficacy and crime. In the final model, collective efficacy was found to completely moderate the relationship between locus of control and crime, but not in the expected direction. After controlling for collective efficacy, the significant negative relationship between locus of control and crime is no longer significant. Areas of future research and implications for theory and policy are discussed.

Acknowledgements

Many people have supported me throughout this endeavor. John Laub, Ray Paternoster, Doris Layton MacKenzie, Alex Piquero, Sally Simpson, and Kenneth Beck provided valuable feedback and guidance on the development and completion of this project. Special thanks to John Laub and Ray Paternoster for challenging my thinking and helping me to grow as a scholar and researcher; and Doris Layton MacKenzie for opening my eyes to the concept of locus of control. On a personal note, I would not have been able to work on this research without the enduring support of William and Christine Ahlin. Lastly, I am indebted to Matthew Payne for his unwavering and unconditional love and understanding during all of my endeavors and to Sarah Payne for making it all worthwhile.

I extend many thanks to Leo Balk of LFB Scholarly and Nicholas Lovrich, the series editor, for this opportunity and to Laurie Tomasino-Rosales for her assistance with formatting.

CHAPTER ONE

The Importance of Locus of Control and Collective Efficacy

Criminological research and explanations of crime and delinquency exist at both the micro- and macro-level. Micro-level investigations examine differences in behaviors within and between individuals. Macro-level work, on the other hand, focuses on patterns in larger systems such as population groups (e.g., neighborhoods). Most criminological research examines the effects of micro- *or* macro-level variables on crime. The inclusion of both micro- and macro-level variables in research attempting to explain criminal behavior occurs less frequently (Tonry, Ohlin, and Farrington, 1991; Wikström and Sampson, 2003).

Inquiries into the interplay between micro- and macro-level variables are important. Macro-level contexts such as the neighborhood provide the ecological basis for human development, and human behavior is affected by both individual and macro-level factors (Elder, 1994, 1995). Individuals are nested in social contexts (Bronfenbrenner, 1979; Cook, 2003; Hitlin and Elder, 2007; Sampson and Laub, 1995; Thomas and Znaniecki, 1918-1920) and their choices are situated in the environment (Hitlin and Elder, 2007; Laub and Sampson, 2003). The contextual setting also influences individuals' behavior (Elder, 1995; Silbereisen and Eyferth, 1986; Thomas and

Znaniecki, 1918-1920; Wikström and Loeber, 2000). As a result, behavior is a function of the interaction between an individual and his or her environment (Bronfenbrenner, 1979, 1992; Lewin, 1935). Silbereisen and Eyferth (1986: 4) describe this interaction as "development as action in context," with action pertaining to "behavior that can be interpreted as a means to achieving certain goals" (see also Wikström, 2004, 2006). Examining both individual- and macro-level variables simultaneously enhances our understanding of behavior and choices, including involvement in crime.

Locus of control is a micro-level concept in social psychology. Locus of control can be internal or external (Rotter, 1966) and this orientation is influenced by the environment (Lefcourt, 1982; Twenge, Zhang, and Im, 2004). Internal control is a person's belief that life circumstances are under their control and are the result of their own actions (or inactions). External control is the belief that much of what happens to a person is beyond their control and is not directly related to their behavior. Locus of control is best described as a continuum and persons are believed to have tendencies towards one end or the other, but they can display traits from either side of the spectrum (see Lefcourt, 1982; Reynolds, 1976).

Rotter's concept of locus of control stems from his conceptualization of social learning theory and the idea of expectations for reinforcement (see Rotter, 1954). Reinforcement, or outcome, is the result of an act or behavior. An individual's beliefs about his or her own locus of control determine these reinforcement expectations. Individuals with an internal locus of control believe that they directly influence outcomes associated with behavior; whereas those with an external locus of control expect fate, chance, or other forces outside of themselves to be the cause of outcomes resulting from their behavior. Internal and external controls influence how an individual behave through these generalized expectations of reinforcement.

Collective efficacy, a macro-level indicator of community context, is a group's perceived ability to control or produce outcomes (Bandura, 2000). In criminology, collective efficacy is composed of two constructs: informal social control and social cohesion (Sampson, Raudenbush, and Earls, 1997). Informal social control pertains to the shared expectation and ability of community members to enforce norms and take action to maintain social order. Social cohesion is defined as mutual trust and shared values among community members. Neighborhoods with high levels of collective efficacy provide increased levels of collective supervision (Kornhauser, 1978; Leventhal and Brooks-Gunn, 2000; Sampson and Groves, 1989) which also increases levels of positive role models (Leventhal and Brooks-Gunn, 2000; Mayer and Jencks, 1989; Molnar, Cerda, Roberts, and Buka, 2008).

Scholars have used locus of control and collective efficacy independently to explain behaviors, including individual-level involvement in crime and delinquency (e.g., Browning, 2002; Cole and Kumchy, 1981; Duke and Fenhagen, 1975; Graham, 1993; Kirk, 2008, 2009; Lederer, Kielhofner, and Watts, 1985; Marsa, O'Reilly, Carr, Murphy, O'Sullivan, Cotter, and Hevey, 2004; Molnar, Miller, Azrael, and Buka, 2004; Obitz, Oziel, and Unmacht, 1973; Parrott and Strongman, 1984) and violence at the neighborhood level (e.g., Browning, 2002; Maxwell, Garner, and Skogan, 2011; Sampson and Raudenbush, 1999; Sampson et al., 1997). However, the concepts of locus of control and collective efficacy have not been studied in concert to explain individual involvement in crime. The current investigation uses multilevel data to examine the relationship between these two variables to further explanations of youth involvement in crime.

To begin, this research explores the relationship between youths' locus of control and their involvement in crime (defined here as self-reported violence, drug dealing, and trouble with police). An internal locus of control, on its own, should be negatively related to involvement in these behaviors. An internal locus of control is likened to having a sense of control over one's future and the choices he or she makes (Rotter, 1966). People with an internal locus of control tend to have personality traits such as responsibility, tolerance, and a general sense of well-being (Hersch and Scheibe, 1967). Having an internal locus of control is also linked to academic achievements and success (Bursik and Martin, 2006; Lynch, Hurford, and Cole, 2002; Nowicki and Roundtree, 1971; but see Graffeo and Silvestri, 2006).

Individuals with an external locus of control are more likely to experience anxiety (Kilpatrick, Dubin, and Marcotte, 1974; Morelli, Krotinger, and Moore, 1979) and depression (Mirowsky and Ross, 1990). They also have lower self-control (Karabenick and Srull, 1978; Mischel, Zeiss, and Zeiss, 1974), are less able to cope with stressful situations (Krause and Stryker, 1984; Sandler and Lakey, 1982), and are less likely to have a general sense of well-being (Larson, 1989) than those whose locus of control leans towards the internal end of the spectrum.

Individuals believing they are in control of their lives should be able to resist involvement in detrimental behavior and be certain that they can successfully pursue more prosocial behaviors (see Ludwig and Pittman, 1999). Having an internal locus of control is one possible explanation why youths refrain from crime. Individuals with an internal locus of control have greater resilience (Efta-Breitbach and Freeman, 2004), self-control (see Gierowski and Rajtar, 2003), and are better equipped to handle stressful situations (Reitzel and Harju, 2000). Further, perceptions of control are positively associated with opportunities and choices (Lefcourt, 1982). As described by Rotter (1966: 2), "A generalized attitude, belief, or expectancy regarding the nature of the causal relationship between one's own behavior and its consequences might affect a variety of behavioral choices in a broad band of life situations." Persons with an internal locus of control have increased opportunities and choices available to them and are more "cautious and calculating about their choices" (Lefcourt, 1976: 52) which may include alternatives to crime. Alternatively, an external locus of control may contribute to involvement in crime and delinquency because these individuals lack resilience, self-control, and positive coping mechanisms in response to stress. The extant literature on the relationship between locus of control and crime is limited and inconclusive. Many studies on this topic are outdated and have methodological limitations that may mask the true relationship between these variables (see Foglia, 2000; Hollin, 1989). The research examining the relationship between locus of control and crime has focused on minor delinquency such as shoplifting (Kelley, 1996), status crimes like truancy (Duke and Fenhagen 1975; Lau and Leung, 1992), aggression (Halloran, Doumas, John, and Margolin, 1999), and chronic behavior problems (Miller, Fitch, and Marshall, 2003). Other studies include only offenders without examining control or comparison groups (e.g., Biggs, Bender, and Foreman, 1983; Bowen and Gilchrist, 2006; Cole and Kumchy, 1981; Cross and Tracy, 1971; Dekel, Benbenishty, and Amram, 2004; Hains and Herrman, 1989; Obitz, Oziel, and Unmacht, 1973; Ollendick and Hersen, 1979). Research studies that include comparison groups are limited by small numbers of participants and convenience samples (e.g., Duke and Fenhagen, 1975; Graham, 1993; Langdon and Talbot, 2006; Lederer, Kielhofner, and Watts, 1985; Marsa, O'Reilly, Carr, Murphy, O'Sullivan, Cotter, and Hevey, 2004; Parrott and Strongman, 1984; Peiser and Heaven, 1996).

Locus of control was a popular research topic during the 1960s and 1970s. While its popularity has waned, scholars (particularly in the field of education) continue to examine this concept as a factor in a variety of behaviors. However, criminology and criminal justice research on the subject has moved away from examining locus of control as an etiological basis of crime. Criminologists continue to investigate locus of control but more often examine how it relates to coping ability among victims of crime (Caputo and Brodsky, 2004; Houts and Kassab, 1997; Thompson and Norris, 1992) and inmate adaptation to prison (Griffith, Pennington-Averett, and Bryan,

1981; LeBlanc and Tolor, 1972; Levenson, 1975; MacKenzie, Goodstein, and Blouin, 1987; Pugh, 1993; Reitzel and Harju, 2000). This research seeks to reexamine locus of control as a mechanism to explain youths' choice to refrain from serious crimes (e.g., violence, drug dealing, and being in trouble with the police).

A second area of interest is the influence of collective efficacy on crime. At the macro-level, collective efficacy has been shown to be negatively related to violent crime rates (Maxwell, Garner, and Skogan, 2011; Sampson et al., 1997) and intimate partner homicide rates (Browning, 2002). At the individual-level, research has demonstrated that higher levels of collective efficacy are associated with lower levels of nonlethal intimate partner violence (Browning, 2002), prevalence of carrying concealed firearms (Molnar, Miller, Azrael, and Buka, 2004), and arrest (Kirk, 2009). It is expected that in this study there will be a negative relationship between collective efficacy and youth involvement in violence, drug dealing, and trouble with police.

Research examining the influence of collective efficacy on antisocial outcomes originally focused on crime rates (e.g., Sampson et al., 1997). More recently, researchers have examined the influence collective efficacy may have on individual-level outcomes (e.g., Kirk, 2008, 2009; Molnar et al., 2008; Sampson, Morenoff, and Raudenbush, 2005; Sharkey, 2006; Simons, Simons, Burt, Brody, and Curtrona, 2005). While some researchers examining collective efficacy have investigated antisocial outcomes such as arrest, delinquency, and aggression, scholars have primarily examined the influence of collective efficacy on violent crime. The current study examines individual-level involvement in violent crime and also includes drug dealing and trouble with police as additional outcomes.

Finally, this research investigates whether collective efficacy moderates the relationship between locus of control and crime. Independently, an internal locus of control and higher levels of collective efficacy are believed to be related to less involvement in crime. It is expected that locus of control and collective efficacy will jointly influence youths' involvement in crime. It is anticipated that the relationship between an internal locus of control and crime will be strengthened among youths living in neighborhoods with higher levels of collective efficacy.

The relationship between locus of control and collective efficacy has not been studied. Scholars have examined the relationship between a similar concept, self-efficacy, and collective efficacy (Fernández-Ballesteros, Díez-Nicolás, Caprara, Barbaranelli, and Bandura, 2002; Sharkey, 2006). Self-efficacy and locus of control, however, are distinct concepts even though they are often thought to be the same variable measured at different levels of specificity where self-efficacy is a domain specific construct and locus of control is more general in nature (Bandura, 1997). The fundamental difference between these concepts relates to the expectations of actions and outcomes. Self-efficacy is concerned with the ability to perform an action while locus of control pertains to how actions affect outcomes. People use their self-efficacy beliefs to make decisions about their behavior (e.g., action). Locus of control is a factor as that person develops expectations of what will occur as a result of that behavior (e.g., outcome). For example, a youth may think that they have the self-efficacy to engage in a crime. The outcome of that crime, being arrested or not, and whether it is attributed to their behavior or forces beyond their control, is dependent on the orientation of their locus of control.

Another important difference is that, unlike locus of control, self-efficacy is generally believed to vary across life domains (Bandura, 1986; but see Agnew and White, 1992; Hoeltje, Zubrick, Silburn, and Garton, 1996; Jerusalem and Mittag, 1995; Jerusalem and Schwarzer, 1992; Pearlin, Menaghan, Lieberman, and Mullan, 1981; Pearlin and Schooler, 1978; Scholz, Doña, Sud, and Schwarzer, 2002; Schwarzer and Born, 1997; Tipton and Worthington, 1984). A person can feel highly efficacious in one area of life, while perceiving him- or herself to be inefficacious in others. Perceptions of locus of control are not tied to specific realms or life domains; they can vary across situations (Rotter, 1966). In fact, omnibus measures are traditionally used to quantify internal or external orientation.[1] Because self-efficacy and locus of control are conceptually different, the two studies investigating the relationship between self-efficacy (Fernández-Ballesteros et al., 2002; Sharkey, 2006)[2] and collective efficacy do not indicate whether expectations related to outcomes (locus of control) influence involvement in crime. Further, they do not assess the moderating effect of collective efficacy on this relationship. Therefore, this study adds to the research literature by expanding the scope of prior work in this area by investigating the relationships between locus of control, collective efficacy, and crime.

In addition, constructs that may influence involvement in crime, locus of control, and collective efficacy are examined as control variables. These are neighborhood context, family context, and individual-level demographics. As stated earlier, there is a relationship between individuals and their environment and neighborhood context influences behavior (Anderson, 1999; Sampson and Bartusch, 1998). Neighborhood context is the environment in which a youth lives and it plays a role in determining whether locus of control orientations affect choices and opportunities (Lefcourt, 1982). It also influences an individual's "perception of alternatives" to involvement in crime (Wikström and Loeber, 2000: 1110; see also Wikström, 2004, 2006) and may have an effect on neighborhood levels of collective efficacy (see Sampson and Bartusch, 1998). In order to account for neighborhood-level factors that may influence the relationships between locus of control, collective efficacy, and crime, and the potential moderating effect of collective efficacy on the relationship between locus of control and crime, neighborhood context constructs (measured at the aggregate level) are incorporated into the analyses as control variables. In this study, neighborhood context is categorized in terms of residential mobility, socioeconomic status, ethnic heterogeneity, and rate of family disruption. These variables are typically used by scholars engaged in ecological research to describe neighborhood context and are described further in Chapters 2 and 3.

Family context may also influence locus of control and collective efficacy, and is an important determinant of involvement in crime (Bronfenbrenner, 1986a; Burton and Jarrett, 2000; Duncan and Aber, 1997; Klebanov, Brooks-Gunn, Chase-Lansdale, and Gordon, 1997; Leventhal and Brooks-Gunn, 2000; Loeber and Stouthamer-Loeber, 1986; Sampson, 1992; Sampson and Morenoff, 1997; Wells and Rankin, 1991). Similar to neighborhood context, the family provides a social context for youth and it influences their development, behavior, and choices. Locus of control orientation has been associated with parenting styles, family environment, and characteristics of parents (Lynch, Hurford, and Cole, 2002; Reynolds, 1976) and families may influence youths' perceptions of their locus of control. Further, family context may influence involvement in crime by contributing to the amount of time a parent can spend with their child, whether his or her behavior is monitored, and availability to serve as a positive role model. Families also contribute to the larger neighborhood social fabric and environment that influences levels of collective efficacy. The family context constructs included in this study as control variables are measured at the individual respondent level and provide information on youths' primary caregivers immigrant status, socioeconomic status, family disruption, family size, and parental monitoring. These constructs are explicated in appropriate detail in Chapters 2 and 3.

Contextual variables such as neighborhood and family are important, but can only explain a portion of individuals' behaviors and choices. Behaviors and choices are also influenced by individual-level factors such as age or cohort membership, sex, and race/ethnicity. These demographics can influence the development of locus of control and involvement in crime and are examined in this study as control variables.

Examining the relationship between locus of control and collective efficacy is important primarily because an individual's actions, including involvement in crime, cannot solely be explained by individual or environmental factors alone; both need to be considered (Wikström, 2006). Combining micro- and macro-levels of explanation in a contextual analysis (see Sampson, 1992) can provide linkages between processes and causal mechanisms of crime (Wikström, 2004) and lead to a more comprehensive explanation of behavior.

The current investigation contributes to the literature by examining the relationships between locus of control and collective efficacy and youths' involvement in violence, drug dealing, and trouble with police, as well as the influence of contextual and individual-level control variables on these relationships. To do this, first the relationship between crime and locus of control is examined. Neighborhood context, family context, and individual-level factors believed to influence involvement in crime are then explored as control variables. Second, the relationship between crime and collective efficacy is explored. It is anticipated that neighborhood context and family context will influence the relationship between collective efficacy and crime and the simultaneous influences of these control variables are explored in an additional model (see Bronfenbrenner, 1979, 1992; Elliott et al., 2006). Once the relationships between locus of control and crime, collective efficacy and crime, and the influence of the control variables on these relationships are established, the moderating influence of collective efficacy on the relationship between locus of control and crime is investigated. To begin, the relationship between locus of control and collective efficacy is examined. Next, the moderating effect of collective efficacy on the relationship between locus of control and crime is explored. Finally, all control variables (neighborhood context, family context, and individual-level factors) are incorporated into a model to assess the moderating effect of collective efficacy on the relationship between locus of control and crime.

The remaining chapters of this book detail the research. In Chapter 2, I discuss the theoretical foundation for exploring the relationships between locus of control, collective efficacy, and control variables, and the potential influence of these constructs on youth involvement in crime. Chapter 3 presents the data and methods used in the analyses. Chapter 4 contains the results from the models investigating the independent influence of locus of control and collective efficacy on crime, models examining the relationships between locus of control, collective efficacy, and the control variables and their influence on crime, and models exploring whether collective efficacy moderates the relationship between locus of control and crime. Finally, Chapter 5 offers a discussion of the findings and examines the implications of these results for future research, theory, and policy.

CHAPTER TWO

Theoretical Considerations

LOCUS OF CONTROL

Locus of control is a concept from social psychology. It pertains to an individual's "beliefs about whether actions affect outcomes" (Bandura, 1997: 20). Locus of control is the idea that actions are predicted by expectations related to outcomes and the current situation (Lefcourt, 1976). It is a continuum ranging from internal to external. As Rotter (1990: 489) states, "Internal versus external control refers to the degree to which persons expect that a reinforcement or an outcome of their behavior is contingent on their own behavior or personal characteristics versus the degree to which persons expect that the reinforcement or outcome is a function of chance, luck, or fate, is under the control of powerful others, or is simply unpredictable."

Locus of control is rooted in Rotter's conceptualization of social learning theory which has four main components: (1) behavior potential; (2) expectancy; (3) reinforcement value; and (4) psychological situation (Rotter, 1954; Lefcourt, 1976). Behavior potential is the likelihood that an individual will partake in a behavior. Expectancy is the subjective probability that the behavior will result in an outcome. Reinforcement value is simply the anticipated outcome resulting from the behavior. Psychological situation encompasses subjectivity and the environment. Locus of control is most concerned with the first three. According to locus of control, behavior potential is a function of expectancies regarding outcomes and the value placed on this reinforcement. In other words, locus of control beliefs determine reinforcement expectations relate to outcomes and these expectations determine behavior.

It is believed that youths with an internal locus of control will be less likely to engage in criminal behavior because they feel more in control of their lives, feel as if they can achieve goals through their own volition, and are able to enact personal control over situations that will lead to desired outcomes. Individuals with an internal locus of control have developed self-regulation that assists them as they make decisions and guide their own life course. Ludwig and Pittman (1999: 462) summarize this idea by stating that "...adolescents who perceive themselves as likely to succeed at socially valued behavior are less likely to be involved in problem behaviors and more likely to make decisions that result in positive consequences." Those who have an internal locus of control will also assume that their behavior will be directly related to outcomes such as success associated with prosocial behavior.

Locus of control is one possible explanation for behavior. As investigated in this study, individuals with an internal locus of control, in connection with the resources and role models available in their environment, may make choices to refrain from crime. Individuals with an internal locus of control have a greater sense of control over outcomes which influences their behavior (Lefcourt, 1976). They are also more likely to set goals for themselves that require self-control and delayed gratification (Lefcourt, 1976) - characteristics associated with having an internal locus of control. Further, those with an internal locus of control enjoy higher academic achievement and better wages in the labor market (Findley and Cooper, 1983; Lefcourt, 1972). On the other hand, people who have an external locus of control will be less likely to reach for positive goals, perhaps due to learned helplessness (see Seligman, 1975) or a sense of fatalism (Wheaton, 1983). They may choose to engage in crime because they do not feel they have control over their life and they believe any outcomes related to their behavior are a function of factors beyond their control.

An external locus of control has been shown to be predictive of involvement in delinquency and crime (Lau and Leung, 1992; Obitz, Oziel, and Unmacht, 1973; Peiser and Heaven, 1996; Rotter, 1966). In general, delinquent girls (Duke and Fenhagen, 1975) and delinquent boys (Parrott and Strongman, 1984) have more external orientations than nondelinquent youths. As noted in Chapter 1, many studies note the significant relationship between minor delinquencies and an external locus of control. Very few scholars have studied the influence of locus of control orientation on more serious crimes. In one exception, Marsa and colleagues (2004) examined locus of control among small samples of child sex offenders, violent offenders, nonviolent offenders, and a community control group. The child sex offenders reported greater externality than the other groups, and violent offenders had a more external orientation than the community control group. Similarly, in a study by Graham (1993), a sample of sex offenders (mostly child sex offenders) was found to rate as external on locus of control measures more often than criminals whose offenses did not involve sexual acts or behavior.[1]

Locus of control also influences coping ability (Rotter, 1966). Several studies have investigated locus of control as it relates to the coping skills of inmates during incarceration and after release. MacKenzie and her colleagues (1987) found that inmates with a greater sense of control were less stressed and were better able to adapt to incarceration (see also Pugh, 1993; Reitzel and Harju, 2000). Among a small sample of juvenile delinquents serving time for their crimes, those with an internal locus of control were less likely than externals to recidivate after release (Ollendick and Hersen, 1979). Other vulnerable populations such as children, adolescents, and victims of crime are able to feel in control over situations if they have an internal locus of control. Duncan (1996) found that youth with an internal locus of control are better equipped to deal with stressors associated living in violent neighborhoods. Female victims of sexual abuse during childhood who also have an internal locus of control experience less distress than their external counterparts; though differences are not statistically significant (Porter and Long, 1999). This research demonstrates that an internal locus of control aids individuals in taking control over their lives and situations and supports the assertion that an internal locus of control may play a role in prosocial development. Having an internal locus of control enables individuals to exercise control over their life (Reynolds, 1976), access opportunities available to them (Lefcourt, 1982), and use positive coping mechanisms during times of distress (Reitzel and Harju, 2000). Therefore, individuals with an internal locus of control may be better equipped to achieve goals through prosocial means and avoid involvement in crime.

COLLECTIVE EFFICACY

Collective efficacy pertains to the interdependence between individuals and their community (Elder, 1994). General definitions of collective efficacy are the ability of individuals in a neighborhood to maintain order over the community (Sampson et al., 1997) and a group's shared belief that action can be realized through combined efforts (Bandura, 1997). More specifically, collective efficacy is the shared expectations for informal social control in public spaces, and the mutual trust and willingness among individuals to take action in their neighborhood against social ills such as crime (Sampson et al., 1997).

Communities with high levels of collective efficacy can realize their common goals through shared expectations and beliefs and a sense of mutual trust (Bandura, 2000; Sampson et al., 1997). Measures of collective efficacy capture perceptions of informal social control and social cohesion in the neighborhood and collective efficacy is often considered to be a goal-oriented construct. Studies in criminology have examined the relationship between collective efficacy and reductions in behaviors such as violence, arrest, delinquency, and aggression (see Kirk, 2008, 2009; Maxwell et al., 2011; Molnar et al., 2008; Sampson et al., 2005; Sampson et al., 1997; Sharkey, 2006).

Research following Mayer and Jencks' (1989) social control model of neighborhood effects postulates that adults act as role models and influence the behavior and actions of all youths in the community, not just those of their own children, and they also provide supervision and monitoring over youths' behavior (see Coleman, 1990; Sampson, 1992; Sampson and Groves, 1989). By providing informal social control and social cohesion, neighborhoods that are high in collective efficacy have a greater capability to achieve goals such as preventing or reducing crime than those that are low in collective efficacy (Sampson et al., 1997).

Using data from the Project on Human Development in Chicago Neighborhoods (PHDCN), Sampson et al. (1997) quantified collective efficacy by measuring informal social control and social cohesion among 8,782 residents in 343 Chicago neighborhoods. The two constructs were highly correlated, and were combined into a single measure of collective efficacy by aggregating individual-level responses. Sampson and colleagues used this measure to examine the effect of collective efficacy on rates of neighborhood violence. They discovered that neighborhoods with higher levels of collective efficacy had lower rates of violence. This finding was replicated by Maxwell and his colleagues (2011). Additional studies provide support for the use of collective efficacy as an important predictor of crime rates (see Sampson and Raudenbush, 1999) and higher levels of collective efficacy have been shown to be related to a decrease in rates in intimate partner homicide (Browning, 2002) as well as residential burglary and rape (Maxwell et al., 2011). In a meta-analysis of macro-level indicators of crime, Pratt and Cullen (2005) determined that collective efficacy, with an effect size of -0.303, is one of the most robust and promising macro-level predictors of crime rates.

Additional research has examined the influence of collective efficacy on individual-level involvement in crime. Lower levels of collective efficacy are related to increases in arrest (Kirk, 2009), and higher levels of collective efficacy are associated with lower incidences of nonlethal intimate partner violence (Browning, 2002)[2] and lower prevalence of carrying a concealed firearm (Molnar, Miller, Azrael, and Buka, 2004). Communities high in collective efficacy also have a greater number of parents using authoritative parenting practices, lower levels of delinquent behavior, and fewer youth interactions with deviant peers (Simons et al., 2005). Molnar et al. (2008) found that youths ages 11 to 18 living in neighborhoods that had high levels of collective efficacy and were rich in resources (e.g., after school programs, substance abuse treatment centers) had lower scores on delinquency and aggression scales (i.e., Achenbach Child Behavior Checklist).

These studies indicate that increases in collective efficacy have a beneficial impact on individual-level crime, but other research does not support these findings. Collective efficacy has not been found to be a significant predictor of violence (Sampson et al., 2005), arrest (Kirk, 2008), or suspension from school (Kirk, 2009) at the individual-level. Further, Zimmerman and Messner (2011) failed to find a significant relationship between neighborhood levels of collective efficacy and youths' exposure to violent peers. Despite the equivocal findings, it is anticipated that increased collective efficacy will be related to a decrease in individual involvement in crime.

It is also believed that collective efficacy will moderate the relationship between locus of control and crime through the availability of informal social control, a sense of social cohesion, and abundant positive social role models, whose presence should be more likely in neighborhoods with higher levels of collective efficacy. This type of social capital that can facilitate productive action (Coleman, 1990) may strengthen the relationship between locus of control and criminal behavior through feelings of hopefulness (see Frytak, Harley, and Finch, 2003). The availability of social resources such as those found in communities high in collective efficacy may influence youths' choice of responses to stressful situations; to engage in or refrain from crime (see Moos and Holahan, 2003).

RELATIONSHIP BETWEEN LOCUS OF CONTROL, COLLECTIVE EFFICACY, AND CRIME

As reviewed above, an internal locus of control and increased levels of collective efficacy independently reduce involvement in antisocial behaviors. Generally, individuals with higher levels of prosocial individual-level assets (e.g., internal locus of control) and community resources (e.g., collective efficacy) are less likely to engage in undesirable behaviors such as crime (see Scales, 1999). Figure 1 shows that the locus of control and collective efficacy variables are believed to independently influence crime. In this study, locus of control refers to a youth's general perception of his or her expectations regarding outcomes across an omnibus measure of actions. The measure of collective efficacy provides information on informal social control and social cohesion at the neighborhood level. Crime is defined as self-reported involvement in 12 violent crimes and dealing marijuana, cocaine/crack, and/or heroin over the past 12 months, and being in trouble with the police since the previous interview.

Figure 1. Effects of collective efficacy and locus of control on crime

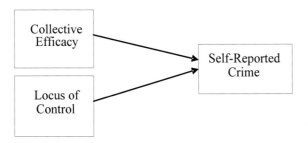

The joint effect of locus of control and collective efficacy on crime is less clear. One of the research questions addressed in this study is whether collective efficacy moderates the relationship between locus of control and crime. Support for cross-level interaction effects on crime exists in the extant literature. Elliott et al. (2006) found that positive parenting practices had a stronger influence on decreasing problem behavior in disadvantaged neighborhoods over the other neighborhood types. In 2009, Kirk investigated the interactive effect of collective efficacy and other informal social controls on student suspension and arrest. He found that school collective efficacy more strongly influences the likelihood of student suspension in neighborhoods with a low level of collective efficacy. Kirk also found support for an interaction effect between collective efficacy and student-teacher trust. Lower levels of student-teacher trust and neighborhood collective efficacy interact and increase the likelihood that students are arrested.

Research incorporating both locus of control and collective efficacy into a single explanation of crime is sparse. To bridge this gap in the literature, I examine the relationship between collective efficacy, locus of control, and crime. Either a moderating or mediating model can be used to examine this relationship. A moderating model (Figure 2) was selected for three reasons. First, it is anticipated that locus of control and collective efficacy are independently related to a reduction in crime. Therefore, a moderator model is appropriate because it is anticipated that collective efficacy will directly influence crime and not influence crime through locus of control.[3] Second, it is believed that the interaction between locus of control and collective efficacy will strengthen the anticipated relationship between locus of control and crime. A moderator model will be used to test whether the combination of two variables (i.e., locus of control x collective efficacy) alters (i.e., weakens, strengthens, renders inconsequential) the relationship between an independent variable (i.e., locus of control) and the outcome (i.e., crime).

Third, Baron and Kenny (1986) suggest that the moderating variable should be uncorrelated to the independent and dependent variables and this is true for the proposed model. Collective efficacy is weakly correlated to locus of control (0.082), violence (0.001), drug dealing (0.011), and trouble with police (0.028). Tangentially, the literature on contextual factors and crime suggests that an interaction effect between macro- and micro-level variables is possible, but it is not known whether one exists between locus of control and collective efficacy. Multilevel models are useful for determining whether individual factors are moderated by macro-level variables (see Taylor, 2010).

Figure 2. Moderator model

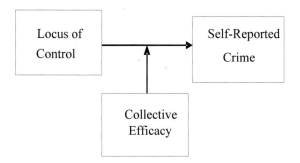

CONTROL VARIABLES

By examining the mesosystem, or multiple contexts, in which people live (Bronfenbrenner, 1979, 1992), information about the interdependency among contexts can be uncovered (see also Kirk, 2009). Individual-level factors also provide important information about people and their behavior and choices. Contextual factors and individual-level factors are important when examining locus of control because they influence the development of an internal or external locus of control. They also influence and inform individual's actions, including involvement in crime. They may also influence the relationships between locus of control, collective efficacy, and crime. Two important contexts (neighborhood and family; see Duncan and Raudenbush, 2001) and three individual-level variables (age/cohort, sex, and race/ethnicity) which influence behavior are examined as control variables in the current research.

Figure 3 provides a visual representation of the conceptual framework. It is based on the ecological literature which envisions individuals as being nested in social contexts at various levels (Bronfenbrenner, 1979). In this study, it is anticipated that an individual's choice to engage in criminal behavior will be influenced by their environment; namely neighborhood context and family context.

Figure 3. Conceptual framework

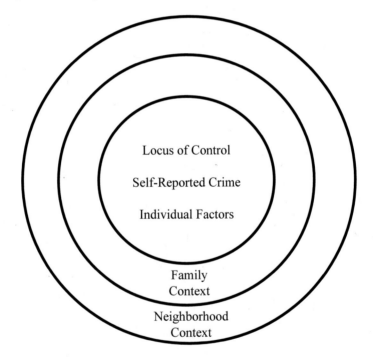

Two other social contexts, school and peers, are also important contextual factors (see Cook, Herman, Phillips, and Settersten, 2002; Elliott et al., 2006; Haynie, 2002; Kirk, 2009; Sampson and Laub, 1993; Warr, 2002) and not including these contexts may result in omitted variable bias (see Duncan and Raudenbush, 2001). However, the focus of this study is on the informal social controls that are exerted through neighborhood and family contexts as a first step in determining if controlling for contextual factors influences the relationship between locus of control and crime.[4] According to Bronfenbrenner (1979), the most direct interactions occur with the family and the neighborhood. Also, the contexts related to schools and peers are not as enduring as neighborhoods and families tend to be traditionally. School environments change as adolescents' age (e.g., transition from elementary school to middle school) and peer affiliations can change rapidly. Neighborhood and family contexts can also change, but they do not tend to change as frequently for most youth.

Neighborhood Context

While individuals have a great deal of influence over their actions and choices, actions and choices are partly the result of the contextual environment (Bronfenbrenner, 1979, 1986b, 1992). Neighborhoods with abundant prosocial resources and role models should provide opportunities that can aid in the development of prosocial cognitive attributes such as an internal locus of control (Fraser, 1996; Frytak, Harley, and Finch, 2003). Impoverished neighborhoods, on the other hand, will have fewer resources and positive role models (Wilson, 1987). They may provide criminal opportunities and role models (Cloward and Ohlin, 1960) and are generally less conducive to the development of an internal attribution style (see Lefcourt, 1982).

Research examining the effects of neighborhood level factors on individual-level offending is an important area for criminological research. These types of studies have been sparse (Farrington, 1993; Wikström and Loeber, 2000), but are steadily growing. Neighborhood context has been shown to be related to a youth's involvement in delinquency (e.g., Wikström and Loeber, 2000) and individual-risk factors such as impulsive behavior and lying interact with neighborhood disadvantage and lead to an increased likelihood of delinquency (Lyman, Caspi, Moffitt, Wikström, Loeber, and Novak, 2000).

One key component of this study is to control for neighborhood factors that may influence the relationships between locus of control, collective efficacy, and crime. Research indicates that neighborhood context influences collective efficacy (see Sampson et al., 1997) and crime (see Wikström and Loeber, 2000). However, less empirical evidence exists for the relationship between neighborhood context and locus of control. The environment is deemed important (Rotter, 1966), but how it influences locus of control is not clear. Other researchers mimic this sentiment and indicate that the environment should influence locus of control beliefs but they do not explicate how this occurs (e.g., Twenge, Zhang, and Im, 2004).

There are many ways to measure neighborhood context. Based on the literature and the available PHDCN data, key data elements were selected to capture neighborhood context for this study. The neighborhood context constructs used in this research are residential mobility, socioeconomic status, ethnic heterogeneity, and family disruption.[5] Neighborhoods that have less residential mobility, a higher socioeconomic status, less ethnic heterogeneity, and lower levels of family disruption should have higher levels of collective efficacy. It is also believed that these neighborhood constructs will influence locus of control. Lefcourt (1982) espouses that a negative environment breeds externality. An internal locus of control is perhaps more likely to develop if resources are plentiful and positive social role models are available to monitor behavior and provide expectancies for prosocial behavior and desirable reinforcement value. Neighborhoods with more of these positive resources and attributes should provide a context which results in an internal locus of control and increased involvement in prosocial behavior. Neighborhood context is measured as residential mobility, socioeconomic status, ethnic heterogeneity, and family disruption. Each is described below.

Residential Mobility

Residential mobility provides a measure of residents' stability in a neighborhood and is indicated by the number of years a person or family lives in a particular neighborhood. Residential stability, defined as people infrequently moving out of the neighborhood, may influence locus of control and collective efficacy. Neighborhoods with lower levels of residential mobility should positively influence the development of an internal locus of control among youths. Youths living in more residentially stable environments should have increased opportunities to develop an internal locus of control through exposure to expectancies and reinforcements provided by steady positive social role models. Additionally, Sampson et al. (1997) indicate that neighborhoods with higher levels of residential mobility are less likely than more stable neighborhoods to have formed informal social control networks and a sense of social cohesion – the two elements that comprise collective efficacy. Further, many studies indicate that higher levels of residential mobility are an important predictor of crime and delinquency (Brooks-Gunn, Duncan, and Aber, 1997a, 1997b; Bursik, 1988; Bursik and Grasmick, 1993; Byrne and Sampson, 1986; Kirk, 2008, 2009; Ross, Reynolds, and Geis, 2000; Sampson, 1992; Sampson and Groves, 1989; Shaw and McKay, 1942; Wikström and Loeber, 2000; Wilson, 1987). Residential mobility decreases the ability of community members to form and activate informal social controls which can lead to increases in crime.

Socioeconomic Status

The overall socioeconomic well-being of a community influences individual development and behavior (Sampson, Morenoff, and Gannon-Rowley, 2002) and may influence the availability of community resources such as collective efficacy (Sampson et al., 1997). It is not clear how the socioeconomic status of a community will influence locus of control. Adults living in neighborhoods with fewer resources may have less opportunity to influence the development of an internal locus of control among youths due to increased stress or constraints on their free time to act as positive role models, monitor youths, and provide reinforcements. Research shows that economic poverty hinders the creation of informal social control and social cohesion; the variables that comprise collective efficacy (Brody, Ge, Conger, Gibbons, Murry, Gerrard, and Simons, 2001; Brooks-Gunn, Duncan, Klebanov, and Sealand, 1993; Gephart, 1997; Gorman-Smith, Tolan, and Henry, 2000; Kirk, 2008, 2009; Sampson, 1992; Sampson and Groves, 1989; Sampson et al., 2002; Shaw and McKay, 1942; Wikström and Loeber, 2000; Wilson, 1987). Neighborhoods low in collective efficacy are also less effective in controlling crime and, because of fewer resources, are less able to supervise youths.

Ethnic Heterogeneity
Ethnic heterogeneity, a mix of people of various races and/or ethnicities, is another neighborhood contextual variable that may influence locus of control, inhibit the development of collective efficacy, and contribute to crime. Two ways through which locus of control is formed are the expectancies that a behavior will lead to a particular outcome and reinforcement value. Youth living in ethnically heterogeneous neighborhoods may be less likely to assimilate and identify with adults in the community, thereby potentially inhibiting positive behavior reinforcements from community members if their behaviors are contrary to the various cultural beliefs and norms evinced by the majority. Thus, ethnic heterogeneity in a neighborhood may act as a barrier to the development of an internal locus of control. It is believed that ethnic heterogeneity in a community leads to weaker and/or fewer informal social controls and social cohesion and this lack of collective efficacy has been shown to lead to increases in crime (Browning and Cagney, 2003; Bursik and Grasmick, 1993; Gorman-Smith et al., 2000; Kirk, 2008, 2009; Sampson, 1992; Sampson and Groves, 1989; Sampson and Morenoff, 1997;

Shaw and McKay, 1942; Wikström and Loeber, 2000; Wilson, 1991).

Family Disruption

Family disruption (e.g., separation/divorce) may influence the development of locus of control and collective efficacy, and involvement in crime. Like the other neighborhood context variables examined here, the relationship between family disruption and locus of control is not evident. As with the other measures, it is anticipated that higher levels of family disruption would result in fewer positive role models to provide expectancies and reinforcement value which assist in the development of an internal locus of control. Family disruption negatively influences the development of collective efficacy (Sampson, 1992; Sampson and Groves, 1989; Sampson and Morenoff, 1997; Shaw and McKay, 1942; Wikström and Loeber, 2000; Wilson, 1987). Higher levels of family disruption may make it less likely that informal social control and social cohesion will develop due to fewer adults residing in the neighborhood to form social networks, supervise youths, and enforce social norms. Family disruption can also lead to less available time by adults to engage in these activities because resources are less abundant. As with the other neighborhood context variables examined, family disruption can lead to low levels of collective efficacy which may contribute to increases in crime and delinquency.

Summary of Neighborhood Context Measures

It is anticipated that these neighborhood context constructs will influence an individual's locus of control orientation and they are known to influence collective efficacy and crime. Neighborhoods with high levels of residential mobility, ethnic heterogeneity, and family disruption, and a lower socioeconomic status may have fewer positive social role models, lower levels of monitoring, and be less likely to provide supportive environments that can provide prosocial expectancies and reinforcement values thought to be essential to the development of an internal locus of control. These neighborhood characteristics also impede the development of collective efficacy and are known to be related to increased involvement in crime. In this study, these neighborhood context constructs are examined as control variables that may influence the relationships between locus of control, collective efficacy, and crime.

Family Context

Families provide an important context for human development (e.g., see Bronfenbrenner, 1986a; Cook et al., 2002; Duncan and Aber, 1997; Furstenberg et al., 1999; Klebanov et al., 1997; Leventhal and Brooks-Gunn, 2000; Loeber and Stouthamer-Loeber, 1986; Sampson, 1992). According to Bronfenbrenner (1979), the family (like the neighborhood) is one of the microsystems in which individuals live and have their most direct interactions with other persons who can influence their thoughts, actions, and behaviors. Further, Leventhal and Brooks-Gunn (2000) indicate that family context has a stronger influence on child outcomes than neighborhood context.

As the primary agents of socialization and monitoring, the family plays a key role in the development of a youth's locus of control (Chance, 1965; Lefcourt, 1976). Lynch, Hurford, and Cole (2002) discuss how parents can influence their children's perceptions and ability to handle situations and how this can impact locus of control orientation. A harsh and rejecting family environment is more prone to encourage an external locus of control through reinforcements that are inconsistent (see Phares, 1976). A study examining the influence of the family on self-reported delinquency provides support for these ideas. Peiser and Heaven (1996) found that a positive family environment (e.g., family is a source of comfort and members are mutually supportive) was negatively related to having an external locus of control. The inverse was also identified: a negative family environment was positively related to an external locus of control.

Families are embedded in the larger community (Sampson, 1992), contribute to the resources that are available (such as collective efficacy), and "act as advocates or brokers for their children's receipt of [these] community resources" (Leventhal and Brooks-Gunn, 2000: 322). Neighborhoods with higher levels of collective efficacy are more likely to have prosocial resources for use by youths and their families. In neighborhoods where resources are low, family context can act as a protective factor (Elliott et al., 2006; Furstenberg et al., 1999).

Measures of family context are important predictors of crime and delinquency (see Farrington, 1993: 22) and are indicators of informal social control and socialization. In a meta-analysis, Loeber and Stouthamer-Loeber (1986) examined several family factors to determine which ones were predictive of and associated with juvenile delinquency. They found that the best predictors were socialization variables such as a lack of parental supervision and parent involvement with the child. Living in a single parent home was also predictive of delinquency, but not as strongly.

Based on the literature and available PHDCN data, the following family context constructs are examined in the analyses: immigrant status, socioeconomic status, family disruption, family size, and parental monitoring. Appendix Table 1A presents a correlation matrix of locus of control and the family context variables.

Immigrant Status

It is not clear how family immigrant status may affect a youth's locus of control orientation. However, as found in work by Sampson and Laub (1993), youths of immigrant families (i.e., youths who are children of a first generation immigrant) may spend less time under greater supervision of their parents. A decrease in monitoring may influence the development of an external locus of control as it may impact perceptions related to expectancies and reinforcement values. Additionally, it could be that due to differences in cultural norms and values, youths of immigrant parents have less interaction with community members, who may otherwise provide an added layer of social support and opportunities for generalized expectancies and reinforcements. These attributes may influence the development of an external locus of control and a sense of powerlessness over outcomes (see Dalgard, Thapa, Hauff, McCubbin, and Syed, 2006).

Community-level studies have shown that neighborhoods with higher levels of immigrants have lower levels of informal social control and collective efficacy and increased levels of violence (Maimon and Browning, 2010; Silver and Miller, 2004; see also Shaw and McKay, 1942). At the individual-level, immigrant status does not appear to be a risk factor for crime. Youths in first or second generation immigrant families are less likely to be arrested than other youths (Kirk, 2008), and youths from any immigrant family (especially those living in the United States 6 years or less) are less likely than native youths to report lifetime use of alcohol and marijuana (Blake, Ledsky, Goodenow, and O'Donnell, 2001). Similarly, Sampson and Laub (1993) indicate that parents' immigrant status (i.e., one or both parents born outside of the United States) does not have a direct effect on youths' involvement in official delinquency.

Socioeconomic Status
Socioeconomic status (SES) is another measure of family context that can influence locus of control (Kelley, 1996), collective efficacy (Sampson et al., 1997), and crime (Burton and Jarrett, 2000; Duncan, Brooks-Gunn, and Klebanov, 1994; Elliott et al., 2006; Kirk, 2008). Results from Kelley's (1996) study of at-risk youth indicate that youths from low income families are more likely to present with an external locus of control (see also Battle and Rotter, 1963; Reynolds, 1976). Related to SES, parents' education level can also influence parental style and the development of locus of control. Youths whose parents have a graduate degree are more likely to have an internal locus of control than those whose parents have a high school education or college degree (Lynch, Hurford, and Cole, 2002). In this study, it is expected that locus of control

orientation will be more external among youths living in families with a lower SES due to fewer available resources and opportunities to monitor behavior and provide desirable expectancies or reinforcements for outcomes. Low SES families may have less time to monitor children's behavior or provide reinforcement because they are often working one or more jobs or experience economic stressors. Families with more resources (e.g., financial, education) have more to invest in their children and those who can afford to, may choose to live in neighborhoods that have higher levels of collective efficacy, less crime, and more prosocial role models.

Similar to neighborhood SES, family SES may contribute to the level of collective efficacy in a neighborhood. Low SES families may have less time and fewer resources to expend in the community which may affect levels of collective efficacy in their neighborhood. Similarly, families with a higher SES may positively contribute to the formation of collective efficacy because they have more resources, such as time, to supervise youths.

In addition to influencing locus of control and collective efficacy, family SES is negatively related to antisocial behaviors such as delinquency, arrest, and conduct disorder (Farrington, 1993; Kirk, 2008; Loeber, Green, Keenan, and Lahey, 1995; but see Elliott et al., 2006). Individuals from lower SES families are more likely than youths from higher SES families to engage in crime. For example, a significant relationship between low family SES and male youth involvement in violence has been demonstrated (Fabio, Tu, Loeber, and Cohen, 2011; but see Maimon and Browning, 2010). It is expected that this finding will be replicated in this study.

Family Disruption
Family disruption (e.g., single-parent household, divorce) is another important measure of family context (Kupersmidt, Griesler, DeRosier, Patterson, and Davis, 1995; McLeod, Kruttschnitt, and Dornfeld, 1994; Sampson, 1987; Wells and Rankin, 1991; Wikström and Loeber, 2000). The influence of

family disruption on delinquency is not necessarily due to the consequences and stressors associated with being a single-parent such as poorer home quality (e.g., enjoyment, conflict) (see Van Voorhis, Cullen, Mathers, and Garner, 1988). Two-parent families are more likely than single-parent families to have more time to monitor their children's behavior and act as a positive role model to provide context for expectancies and reinforcement value. This is because they can share parenting and other household duties. Research suggests that parental influence is important to the development of an internal locus of control. Youths not living with their natural parents are more likely to develop an external locus of control (see Kelley, 1996). Youths experiencing the divorce of their parents may feel less in control of their life circumstances than other youths (see Twenge et al., 2004). It is expected that youths living in a two-parent household will have greater internality of locus of control and lower levels of crime than youths in disrupted families.

Family disruption leads not only to fewer adults available to adequately monitor youths and aid in the development of an internal locus of control among children in one's own family, but as discussed earlier, it also limits the number of adults who can enforce social norms in the community (see Gottfredson and Hirschi, 1990; Sampson and Laub, 1993). Family disruption may also influence the development of collective efficacy in a neighborhood. Family disruption may increase the demands and stressors on those who remain in the community, which may inhibit the development of collective efficacy.

Research indicates that family disruption is a predictor of violent offending (Maimon and Browning, 2010), arrest (Kirk, 2008), and delinquency (Juby and Farrington, 2001; Mack, Leiber, Featherstone, and Monserud, 2007; Matherne and Thomas, 2001; Sampson and Groves, 1989; Smith and Jarjoura, 1988; Wells and Rankin, 1991). A meta-analysis of 50 studies shows that juveniles from disrupted families are 10 to 15 percent more likely to become involved in delinquent behavior than youths living in two-parent households (Wells and Rankin,

1991). Further, this review suggests that the effects of a broken home are stronger for minor status offenses such as running away (weighted average effect size = 0.117) than serious crimes such as violence (weighted average effect size = 0.042), theft (weighted average effect size = 0.042), or marijuana/drug use (weighted average effect size = 0.088).

Family Size

Family size is another family context variable explored in this study. The effect of family size on locus of control is not known. A larger family may inhibit the development of an internal locus of control (see Kelley, 1996). One hypothesis is that a larger family size may be associated with additional stressors that could impact expectancies and reinforcements. However, it is also possible that family size will influence locus of control through other family context factors, such as monitoring (see Sampson and Laub, 1993), and the increased availability of expectancies and reinforcement value. Studies suggest that a smaller family size appears best able to contribute to the development of an internal locus of control. Parents of only (or fewer) children may have more time to spend with their child to provide experiences such as increased affection and low exposure to difficult situations (see Katkovsky, Crandall, and Good, 1967; Parrott and Strongmann, 1984) in which the child can develop a sense of responsibility and ownership over their actions.

Family size may also influence collective efficacy at the neighborhood level. More persons residing in a household could contribute to an increase in collective efficacy through the availability of additional agents of informal social control and enforcers of social norms. Neighborhoods with fewer persons may have lower levels of collective efficacy.

Family size is associated with delinquency, though the literature regarding its influence presents a mixed picture. It is anticipated that a larger family provides more opportunities for monitoring and socialization for the prevention of crime.[6] However, a larger number of people living in the household could lead to an increase (Farrington, 1992; Sampson and Laub,

1993; West and Farrington, 1973) or have no effect (Kirk, 2008) on measures of criminal behavior (e.g., arrest, self-report). However, it is anticipated that in this study a larger family size will provide more monitoring of behavior and increased opportunity for expectancies and reinforcements and, thus, be associated with a reduction in crime.

Parental Monitoring

Child rearing practices influence the development of locus of control orientations (Lefcourt, 1976). Parenting methods and attitudes (Lefcourt, 1976) as well as parental expectations of their children for early independence (Chance, 1965) can have an impact on whether a child has internal or external general expectancies. These monitoring and socialization efforts assist children in forming perceptions about their locus of control. As noted in previous sections, families are important for the development of an internal locus of control (Lefcourt, 1976) and families with higher levels of parental supervision and monitoring may provide a prosocial environment where youths can develop the belief that they are able to control their future and steer their own life course.

Parental monitoring may also influence collective efficacy. Monitoring is thought to be a key component of collective efficacy (Kirk, 2008, 2009; Sampson et al., 2002) because adults in neighborhoods high in collective efficacy monitor not only their own children, but all youths. Increases in parental monitoring of one's own child(ren) may spill over to the community and increase informal social control and social cohesion at the neighborhood level.

Poor parental monitoring is one of the most robust correlates of delinquency (Farrington, 1993; Loeber and Stouthamer-Loeber, 1986; Gorman-Smith, Tolan, Zelli, and Huesmann, 1996; Sampson, 1992). Lack of parental monitoring or supervision may provide increased opportunities for youths to engage in crime (see Sampson and Laub, 1993), whereas families with higher levels of monitoring and supervision should provide fewer chances.

Summary of Family Context Measures

It is anticipated that these family context constructs will influence the development of an internal locus of control, collective efficacy, and crime. The influence of immigrant status on locus of control and crime is unknown. However, increases in socioeconomic status and parental monitoring should aid the development of an internal locus of control, while family disruption may encourage an external locus of control. It is not clear how family size is related to locus of control. Family context may also influence collective efficacy. It is expected that increases in socioeconomic status, family size, and parental monitoring would be positively related to collective efficacy, while immigrant status and family disruption may impede its development. In this study, the family context constructs are examined as control variables that may influence the relationships between locus of control, collective efficacy, and crime. Scholars have demonstrated that these family context constructs are associated with criminal behavior and it is expected that similar results will be found in the analyses.

Individual-Level Control Variables

Individual characteristics are also important in explanations of crime and the development of locus of control. The use of only contextual variables in an analysis can lead to misinterpretation of results and attribution of outcomes to contextual characteristics, when results may actually be a result of individual factors. Also, contextual factors may operate differently for various types of individuals. Therefore, youths' age/cohort, sex, and race/ethnicity will be included in the analyses as control variables. Appendix Table 2A presents a correlation matrix to demonstrate the relationship between locus of control and the individual-level control variables.

Age/Cohort

Age is explored as a possible control variable not only because it is a known correlate of crime (Gottfredson and Hirschi, 1990; Hirschi and Gottfredson, 1983), particularly violent crime (see

Maimon and Browning, 2010), but because age may influence locus of control. The extant literature does not consistently find evidence to support a relationship between locus of control and age (Reynolds, 1976). According to Reynolds (1976: 222), individuals develop a "relative stable faith in [their] ability, or lack thereof, to exercise control over the things which happen to" them. However, Lefcourt (1982) suggests that locus of control may become more internal over time as people gain experiences related to expectancies and reinforcements (see also Nowicki and Strickland, 1973).

In this study, age is related to an individual's cohort assignment. The PHDCN uses a multi-cohort accelerated longitudinal research design with youths who have overlapping ages in the various cohorts (Tonry, Ohlin, and Farrington, 1991). In her examination of the National Youth Study, another multi-cohort accelerated longitudinal research study, Lauritsen (1998: 144) suggests that "if estimates of crime involvement...are not significantly different from one another in each of the cohort comparisons, then it is logical to infer that a single development trajectory describes involvement in crime" for the entire age range. To test whether it is necessary to control for cohort in lieu of age in the analyses, analysis of variance (ANOVA) is used to determine whether there are cohort differences in the dependent variables and locus of control. For the three cohorts in the current study, the means of involvement in violence, drug dealing, and trouble with police, and locus of control are not equal ($p < 0.000$) (data not shown). In other words, there are cohort differences with respect to these variables. To control for these differences, cohort will be added to the models that include individual-level factors to account for potential differences in outcomes.

Because age and cohort are highly correlated (0.971), only cohort will be used as a control variable. Controlling for cohort will allow for the influence of neighborhoods and families to be investigated at varying age stages. The influence that neighborhoods have on actions and behavior may be age-graded and as children age they spend less time with their families. Elliott et al. (2006: 4) state that "neighborhood research has shown that ...neighborhood properties ...have different effects on different age groups." Duncan and Raudenbush (2001) also postulate that older children typically spend more time away from home which results in differential exposure to neighborhood contextual influences. While neighborhood effects do not appear to be substantial until ages 16-18, little is known about neighborhood effects during early adolescence, late adolescence, and into early adulthood (Elliott et al., 2006).

Sex

It is well documented that males are more likely than females to be delinquent (Heimer, 2000; Nagin and Paternoster, 1991; Smith and Visher, 1980; Steffensmeier and Allan, 1996; but see Steffensmeier, Schwartz, Zhong, and Ackerman, 2005) and males are more likely to engage in violent crime (Maimon and Browning, 2010). Additionally, the literature notes possible differences in locus of control orientations among males and females, though the research is inconclusive. Most studies do not find significant differences in locus of control orientation between males and females (Reynolds, 1976); however, differences in magnitude may exist. Lau and Leung (1992) found that an external locus of control was related to lower academic expectations in both males and females, but note differences in the source of their sense of external control. According to their study, an external locus of control was significantly related to having a poor parent-child relationship for both sexes, but the effect was stronger for girls. Gender differences in locus of control are also evident among inmates. Griffith, Pennington-Averett, and Bryan (1981) found that women inmates' locus of control did not vary with length of imprisonment; whereas prior literature indicated that male inmates became more external the longer they were incarcerated (LeBlanc and Tolor, 1972; but see Levenson, 1975).

Race/Ethnicity

Like age and sex, race/ethnicity is another variable that is often used in criminological research because the extant literature indicates a differential involvement in crime by various groups. Research shows that compared to other races/ethnicities, African Americans are disproportionately involved in the criminal justice system (see Sampson and Wilson, 1995; Wilson and Herrnstein, 1985). Studies also demonstrate a differential involvement in various types of crimes by minorities. For example, Maimon and Browning (2010) found that being African American is a significant predictor of violent offending.

The literature suggests that there are significant differences between whites and minorities with regard to locus of control. Scholars have indicated that minorities are more likely to have an external locus of control (Reynolds, 1976). However, existing reviews of literature examining race/ethnicity differences in locus of control may suffer from period effects because they were conducted during a period of civil unrest and blatant discrimination (e.g., 1960s and 1970s). Locus of control regarding fear of crime may also differ by race/ethnicity. In their examination of the relationship between fear of crime and locus of control, Houts and Kassab (1997) found that racial/ethnic minorities were more likely than whites to have an external locus of control.

Research on the relationships between race/ethnicity, locus of control, and crime is sparse. Lefcourt and Ladwig (1966) explored locus of control orientations among inmates and found that African Americans had higher levels of externality than the general, nonincarcerated population. White inmates in this study did not significantly differ than the nonincarcerated public. Groh and Goldenberg (1976) obtained similar results. However, these studies suffer from small sample sizes, were conducted over 30 years ago, and do not address the relationship between locus of control and involvement in particular crimes. As previously stated, the findings from these studies may reflect contextual factors of the time (e.g., race relations) that may no longer significantly impact expectancies related to outcomes. This study provides a contemporary look at the relationship between race/ethnicity, locus of control, and crime.

Summary of Individual-Level Measures

These individual-level constructs (age/cohort, sex, and race/ethnicity) are anticipated to influence locus of control and involvement in crime. Older youths may have a greater internal locus of control orientation and those with an internal locus of control should be less likely to engage in crime. Given the extant literature, it is not clear how sex and race/ethnicity will affect locus of control, but it is expected that females and Whites will have an internal locus of control and be less involved in crime than males and minorities.

CHAPTER THREE

Research Hypotheses and Methodology

This study uses data drawn from the Project on Human Development in Chicago Neighborhoods (PHDCN) to examine the influence of locus of control and collective efficacy on youths' involvement in violence, drug dealing, and trouble with police. It also investigates the potential moderating effect of collective efficacy on the relationship between locus of control and these behaviors. Further, contextual and individual-level control variables are examined.

In this chapter, the PHDCN studies and the data collected are described in some detail. Next, the measures used to test the research questions are outlined. Bivariate analyses are then presented to demonstrate the relationship between the outcomes and the family context and individual-level control variables. Finally, the analytic approach employed in this study is discussed.

The following research questions are based on a review of the literature and serve as a guide for exploring the relationships between locus of control, collective efficacy, and crime:

1. Does locus of control influence self-reported involvement in crime?

2. Does collective efficacy influence self-reported involvement in crime?

3. Does collective efficacy moderate the relationship between locus of control and crime?

PHDCN Studies and Data

Using an interdisciplinary approach, the PHDCN sought to examine causal pathways of involvement in prosocial and antisocial behaviors and the influence of neighborhood context on these behaviors. To accomplish this goal, the PHDCN integrated neighborhood level surveys and observations with multiple individual-level surveys of youths and their primary caregivers.

As a result, the PHDCN contains four separate but complimentary studies. The four PHDCN studies are the Community Survey (CS), Longitudinal Cohort Study (LCS), Systematic Social Observations (SSO), and Infant Assessment Unit (IAU). The SSO and IAU studies are not used in the current research and will not be discussed. The CS and LCS are used in this research and are described below.

Community Survey

In 1994-1995, a cross-sectional Community Survey (CS) was conducted to ascertain perceptions of residents living in Chicago.[1] The CS consisted of 8,782 household interviews of adult residents (18 and older) living in Chicago. Participants were identified by sampling residents living in Chicago's 847 census tracts. The census tracts were collapsed into 343 Chicago neighborhood clusters (NC) and each NC contained about 2.3 census tracts and approximately 8,000 residents. The NCs were designed to be "ecologically meaningful" and were constructed using geographically relevant boundaries and first-hand knowledge about the neighborhoods (see Sampson et al., 2002).

The NCs were also representative of Chicago's racial/ethnic and social class diversity. Each NC was stratified on seven racial/ethnic categories and three social classes (Sampson et al., 1997). After the NCs were constructed, a three-stage sampling technique was employed. City blocks were first sampled within each NC. Second, residential dwelling units were sampled within each block. Finally, one adult (18 years of age or older) was selected from each of the sampled dwellings. Approximately 25 residents from each NC were interviewed for the CS.

Using a distinct sample from the other PHDCN studies, the CS serves as an independent measure of community context. For this study, the CS provides individual-level data on collective efficacy and neighborhood context (i.e., residential mobility, socioeconomic status, family disruption) which are aggregated to the NC level.[2] Typically, scholars conducting research using the PHDCN datasets obtain some neighborhood context measures (e.g., percentage of immigrants) from United States census data. Due to the data limitations of the restricted data user's agreement with the Inter-University Consortium for Political and Social Research (ICPSR), some data (e.g., census data) are treated as private in order to prevent respondent identification. These data are not available for use by the public or those who have a restricted data user's agreement with ICPSR. Therefore, proxy measures that closely approximate the census variables are used in this study. All measures used in the study are discussed below under the heading "Measures."

Longitudinal Cohort Study

The Longitudinal Cohort Study (LCS) is a three-wave, multi-cohort, prospective, accelerated longitudinal study of childhood and adolescent development. The LCS sampled youths, young adults, and primary caregivers living in Chicago during 1994. For the LCS, 80 NCs were sampled from the 343 NCs identified for the CS. As with the CS, the 80 NCs selected for the LCS were stratified on racial/ethnic and socioeconomic status (Table 1).

Using a stratified random probability sample, households in Chicago were selected for the LCS in 1994, and 8,347 participants (youths and their primary caregiver) were deemed eligible for the study. Youth participants were allocated to one of seven cohorts and they, and/or their primary caregiver, were interviewed during three waves of data collection. The seven cohorts were labeled according to the respondents' youngest ages at the beginning of the study (Wave 1) which were 0, 3, 6, 9, 12, 15, and 18. Wave 1 data were collected during 1994-1997 and had 6,228 respondents (a 75 percent response rate). During 1997-2000,

Wave 2 data were collected from those who participated in the study during Wave 1 and had not died[3] and had 5,338 respondents (an 86 percent response rate). During 2000-2002, Wave 3 data were collected from those who participated in the study during Wave 1 or Wave 2 and had not died (N = 6,203), and had 4,850 respondents (a 78 percent response rate).

Table 1. Racial/ethnic and socioeconomic status stratification of 80 LCS neighborhood clusters

Racial/Ethnic Stratum	Socioeconomic Status			Total
	Low	Medium	High	
≥70% African American	9	4	4	17
≥70% White	0	4	8	12
≥70% Hispanic	4	4	0	8
≥20% Hispanic; ≥20% White	4	5	4	13
≥20% Hispanic; ≥20% African American	4	4	0	8
≥20% African American; ≥20% White	2	4	4	10
Other	4	5	3	12
Total	27	30	23	80

Letters were mailed informing the study participants that PHDCN research staff would be contacting them to schedule an interview. Data collected at prior Waves were used for tracking purposes. Interviews were conducted in English, Spanish, and Polish, depending on the respondent's language needs and preferences. Participants speaking other languages were administered abbreviated questionnaires. At each Wave, respondents were paid between $5 and $20 for each interview. Other incentives included free tickets to local attractions and prize drawings of $1,000 for participants who kept their original scheduled interview.

Interviews were conducted in-person when possible. Alternatively, participants were interviewed by telephone. As with all longitudinal studies, participants often move between data collection periods. Participants residing outside of the nine counties comprising the Chicago metropolitan area were interviewed using an abbreviated telephone interview. There were 221 telephone interviews during Wave 2 (about 4 percent of the sample).[4] Participants who were in jail or prison (Cook County jail or other state institution) were interviewed in-person if they were detained in the nine-county metropolitan area of Chicago. Individuals and primary caregivers detained outside of this area were interviewed by telephone. During Wave 2, four primary caregivers and two young adults were interviewed in jail. Children in foster care could not be interviewed. Depending on their circumstances at a particular follow-up Wave, some children and primary caregivers may have been interviewed during one Wave but not another.

Individuals in Cohorts 3 through 18 were interviewed personally. In addition to the individual youth respondents, primary caregivers were interviewed for most cohorts.[5] Youth participants who were living away from home (emancipated minors) or were married before the age of 18 were administered any surveys that would have been asked of their primary caregivers, resulting in proxy interviews.

The current study uses LCS data from three cohorts (9, 12, and 15) collected during Wave 1 and Wave 2 and provides individual-level information on youths and their primary caregivers (i.e., self-reported offending, locus of control, family context, and individual-level control variables) and ethnic heterogeneity. These three cohorts were chosen because they were administered the locus of control instrument at Wave 2; the other cohorts were not asked these questions. The locus of control instrument was also administered to Cohorts 9 and 12 at Wave 3, but Wave 2 data were selected for this study because prospective studies are subject to selective attrition (Scott and Alwin, 1998) and one less cohort was administered the survey at Wave 3. By using locus of control data collected at Wave 2 rather than Wave 3, there are 763 additional cases available for study inclusion. The total number of youths in Cohorts 9, 12, and 15 interviewed at Wave 2 was 2,345, and the number of youths administered the locus of control instrument at Wave 2 was 1,914. Table 2 displays the data sources, years of data availability, and the variables by construct.

Table 2. Data source, year of data availability, and constructs
         (variables)

Data Source	Years	Constructs *(Variables)*
<u>Community Survey (CS)</u> *Interviews with 8,782 adult* *residents living in 343* *Chicago neighborhood* *clusters*	1994- 1995	Neighborhood Context: *Collective Efficacy* *Residential Mobility* *Socioeconomic Status* *Family Disruption*
<u>Longitudinal Cohort Study</u> <u>(LCS) - Wave 1</u> *Interviews with 6,228 youths* *and primary caregivers* *living in 80 Chicago* *neighborhood clusters* *Subset included:* *Cohort 9* *Cohort 12* *Cohort 15*	1994- 1997	Neighborhood Context: *Ethnic Heterogeneity* Family Context: *Immigrant Status* *Socioeconomic Status* *Family Disruption* *Family Size* *Parental Monitoring*
<u>Longitudinal Cohort Study</u> <u>(LCS) - Wave 2</u> *Interviews with 5,338 youths* *and primary caregivers* *living in 80 Chicago* *neighborhood clusters* *Subset included:* *Cohort 9* *Cohort 12* *Cohort 15*	1997- 1999	Locus of Control Self-Reported Crime: *Violence* *Drug Dealing* *Trouble with Police* Individual-Level Controls: *Age/Cohort* *Sex* *Race/Ethnicity*

APPROPRIATENESS OF THE PHDCN DATA

The PHDCN data are appropriate for answering the questions addressed in this research for several reasons. First, Chicago is a large city that has significant population heterogeneity. Chicago has diversity among racial and ethnic groups, as well as social classes, and the sampling procedures were stratified using these demographic variables. This diversity will allow the findings to be generalized to various ethnic/racial groups and social classes. Second, the PHDCN data set has a wide range of variables that are applicable to the study's research questions; including self-reported offending, locus of control, collective efficacy, neighborhood context, and family context. Finally, because the PHDCN contains data on individuals who are nested in neighborhood clusters, investigations can be made into the differences between and within neighborhoods.

Data Reduction

Since the analyses examine the influence of locus of control and collective efficacy on crime and the moderating effect of collective efficacy on the relationship between locus of control and crime, it is necessary to limit the analytic file to subjects who have data for these measures. The two data files (CS and LCS) for the three cohorts of interest were merged to determine the completeness of the data for the key variables of interest. Of the 1,914 individuals administered the locus of control instrument, 1,850 have complete data. For the outcome variables, 1,850 have data on the 12 violent acts, 1,880 have data on the 3 drug dealing measures, and 1,907 have data on trouble with police. The final data set was compiled using listwise deletion.[6] The 578 individuals who were deleted from the data set do not differ significantly from the retained individuals with regard to sex ($t = -0.117$, d.f. $= 2,340$, $p > 0.05$), race/ethnicity ($t = -1.30$, d.f. $= 2,013$, $p > 0.05$), or neighborhood collective efficacy ($t = -1.95$, d.f. $= 2,343$, $p > 0.05$). The final sample size, by cohort and sex, is depicted in Table 3.

Table 3. Sample size by cohort and sex

Sex	Cohort			Total
	9	12	15	
Female	276	327	274	877
Male	333	314	243	890
Total	609	641	517	1,767

Individuals with missing data in Cohorts 9 and 15 are not statistically significantly different from individuals in their respective cohorts who have complete data (Cohort 9: $t = 1.58$, d.f. = 2,340, $p > 0.05$; Cohort 15: $t = 0.69$, d.f. = 2,340, $p > 0.05$). However, individuals in Cohort 12 with missing data are different from those in Cohort 12 who have complete data ($t = -2.25$, d.f. = 2,340, $p < 0.05$). The significant differences between those with and without missing data in Cohort 12 may affect the parameter estimates and bias the results.

MEASURES

The dependent variable of interest is self-reported offending, defined as violence, drug dealing, and being in trouble with the police. Locus of control and collective efficacy are independent variables. The control variables are neighborhood context (residential mobility, socioeconomic status, ethnic heterogeneity, and family disruption), family context (immigrant status, socioeconomic status, family disruption, family size, and parental monitoring), and individual-level demographics (age/cohort, sex, and race/ethnicity).

Dependent Variables

Self-Reported Offending
In this study, the dependent variables are three measures of self-reported offending: violence, drug dealing, and being in trouble with the police. Self-report data has been shown to be a valid and reliable method for quantifying delinquency (see Hindelang, Hirschi, and Weis, 1979, 1981; Thornberry and Krohn, 2000). It

also overcomes arrest and reporting biases and probability of detection issues inherent in official data sources (Mosher, Miethe, and Phillips, 2002; Krohn, Thornberry, Gibson, and Baldwin, 2010).

The "Self-Report of Offending" survey administered during Wave 2 to youths in Cohorts 9, 12, and 15 provide data on involvement in crime. In this study self-reported crime is operationalized as involvement in violence in the past 12 months, drug dealing in the past 12 months, and/or being in trouble with police since the Wave 1 interview. The inclusion of a variety of criminal behaviors is supported by the extant literature that indicates a lack of specialization among individuals engaged in crime (Farrington, 1986, 1995, 2003; Gottfredson and Hirschi, 1990, 2003; Hirschi and Gottfredson, 2001; Junger and Deković, 2003; Miethe, Olson, and Mitchell, 2006; Piquero, Paternoster, Mazerolle, Brame, and Dean, 1999; Wolfgang, Thornberry, and Figlio, 1987), particularly youths (Piquero, Farrington, Welsh, Tremblay, and Jennings, 2009).

Table 4. Item wording and descriptive statistics for self-reported violence (past 12 months) scale

Item Wording	N	Percent	St. Dev.
Carried hidden weapon	1,767	6.2	0.241
Purposively damaged property	1,767	8.0	0.272
Set fire	1,767	0.3	0.057
Snatched purse	1,767	0.4	0.062
Hit someone not live with	1,767	18.6	0.389
Attack someone with weapon	1,767	2.6	0.159
Thrown objects at people	1,767	9.8	0.298
Chased someone to scare	1,767	9.7	0.295
Shot someone	1,767	0.3	0.051
Shot at someone	1,767	0.7	0.084
Been in gang fight	1,767	3.6	0.187
Threaten to hurt someone	1,767	4.8	0.214

Scale reliability coefficient: 0.711

Figure 4. Number of violent acts committed in past 12 months

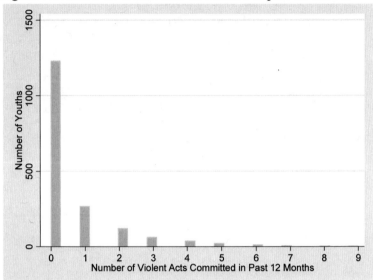

Sharkey's (2006) 12-item violence scale is used for quantifying past year involvement in violent behavior.[7] The survey items were recorded as binary variables (0 = no/1 = yes), combined into a variety scale (Hindelang et al., 1981), and are displayed in Table 4. The scale has high reliability ($\alpha = 0.71$). The violence scale captures the total number of violent offenses committed in the past year by youths. The potential range is 0 to 12, although the actual responses range from 0 to 9 (Figure 4).[8]

The survey inquired about their involvement in drug dealing during the past 12 months. Youths were asked whether they sold marijuana, crack/cocaine, and/or heroin during that time period (Table 5). The range of responses was 0-3, with zero indicating no involvement in drug dealing, 1 and 2 indicating drug dealing of one or two substances, respectively, and 3 indicating the individual sold all three drugs in the past 12 months (Figure 5).

Table 5. Item wording and descriptive statistics for self-reported drug dealing (past 12 months) scale

Item Wording	N	Percent	St. Dev.
Sold marijuana	1,767	3.4	0.178
Sold crack/cocaine	1,767	1.2	0.111
Sold heroin	1,767	0.2	0.041

Scale reliability coefficient: 0.499

Figure 5. Number of different types of drugs dealt in past 12 months

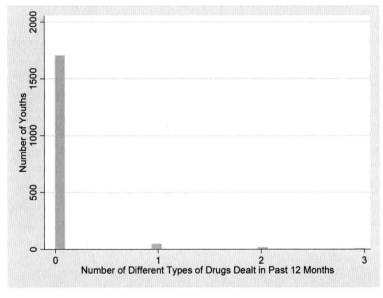

Frequency scores for the violence and drug dealing scales were not generated for several reasons. Foremost, alpha coefficients are more reliable for variety scores than frequency scores (Hindelang et al., 1981). Additionally, variety scores are less skewed than frequency scores, responses about whether an event occurred are more reliable than how many times it occurred, and in variety scores equal weight is attributed to each type of offense instead of more weight being attributed to lesser (and more frequent) behaviors (Moffitt, Caspi, Rutter, and Silva, 2001).

Also examined is a binary variable (0 = no/1 = yes) indicating whether youths had been in trouble with the police since the Wave 1 interview. Of the 1,767 youths in the sample, 13.75% (N = 243) answered yes to the question "Since [Wave 1 interview], have you had any trouble with the police?" (Figure 6). This construct has face validity, and is correlated with the violence scale (0.413) and drug dealing scale (0.248).

Figure 6. Trouble with police since Wave 1 interview

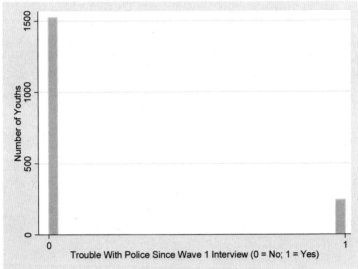

The use of additional self-reported offending behavior (e.g., property crime, traffic offenses) and trouble with other authorities (e.g., courts, schools) was explored but was not practical due to low scale reliabilities, response rates, and extensive missing data problems.

Crime (the dependent variable) is measured at Wave 2 for this research and the time period covered by the self-reported offending questions is the past 12 months for the violence and drug dealing scales, and since the Wave 1 interview (e.g., 1994-1997) for determining trouble with police. The key independent variable, locus of control (discussed below) is also measured at Wave 2 and does not reference a particular time period. The timing of these questions may contribute to temporal ordering concerns, including the effect of locus of control on crime. The relationship between Wave 2 locus of control and Wave 3 self-reported offending is not examined in this research because locus of control can vary over time (Nowicki and Strickland, 1973; see also Twenge et al., 2004) and the relationship between cognitions and outcomes is more explanatory when the two are measured in close proximity and not several years apart after cognitions may have changed. However, to understand the stability in self-reported offending chi-square tests are employed to assess the stability of individuals' involvement in the outcomes of interest between Wave 2 and Wave 3. Responses were dichotomized for the violence and drug dealing scales;[9] where 0 = no involvement in any of the behaviors and 1 = involvement in one or more of the behaviors. Chi-square tests (Table 6) for the three outcome variables indicate both stability and change between Wave 2 and Wave 3.

Table 6. Stability of self-reported offending between Wave 2 and Wave 3

	χ^2	d.f.	Phi
Violence Scale	239.697***	1	0.413***
Drug Dealing Scale	0.068	1	-0.007
Trouble with Police	0.196	1	-0.012

***$p < 0.000$

The chi-square test indicates a moderate positive relationship between violence at Wave 2 and Wave 3 and a weak negative relationship between drug dealing and trouble with police at Wave 2 and Wave 3. The correlations between the crime measures at Wave 2 and Wave 3 are positive and support these findings (violence = 0.519; drug dealing = 0.275; trouble with police = 0.261).[10] As an added measure, the relationship between self-reported involvement in the crimes of interest at Wave 3 and locus of control at Wave 2 is examined to determine the stability of the effect of locus of control on crime, (see Chapter 4).

Independent Variables

Locus of Control
Rotter (1966) developed the Internal-External Locus of Control Scale, or I-E Scale, that asks respondents to indicate how they feel about situations and ideas by choosing between two options. One option is based on individual control (internal locus of control) and the other option emphasizes the involvement of outside forces (external locus of control) over life circumstances. For example, one set of statements on Rotter's scale is:

> *Many of the unhappy things in people's lives are partly due to bad luck.*

> *People's misfortunes result from the mistakes they make.*

The first statement indicates that misfortunes are not under the control of the respondent. People choosing this statement over the other option, and other statements like it, are considered to have an external locus of control. The second statement is indicative of how a person with an internal locus of control would feel about the occurrence of unpleasant situations. The questions on the I-E scale (and other locus of control scales) are indirect indicators. They do not necessarily ask respondents directly about themselves and how they feel about their own lives, though they provide insight into beliefs about where their attitudes about control originate; either internally or externally.

Based on Rotter's work, locus of control has been measured using a number of omnibus scales (for example, the Nowicki-Strickland Locus of Control Scale). Similar to Rotter's I-E scale, these instruments ask respondents to indicate whether they attribute life circumstances and outcomes as being within a person's own control or the result of fate or luck. Responses to a locus of control instrument provide information necessary to make determinations about one's locus of control orientation. Individuals with an internal locus of control perceive themselves as having control over their circumstances and choices while those with an external locus of control believe that outcomes are due to forces beyond their control.

The locus of control data used in this research were collected from Cohorts 9, 12, and 15 during Wave 2 using the survey instrument titled "Things I Can Do If I Try." This 30-item instrument was created by members of the PHDCN scientific group specifically for the PHDCN and has not been validated. Each statement was read to respondents and scored on a Likert-type scale. Each statement offered two perspectives (e.g., "some kids feel like they can understand math if they work at it," BUT "other kids feel no matter how hard they work at it, it is still very hard to learn math"). Similar to Rotter's scale, youth were asked to choose which perspective more closely reflected their perceptions and beliefs about themselves and what they believed to be true, not what they would like to be true.

The measures included positively and negatively worded statements. Regardless of the direction of the question, in the original data set, the responses were coded as "very true," "sort of true," "sort of untrue," and "very untrue" with a value of 1 through 4, respectively. Therefore, the original data set assigned a value of 1 to any response of "very true" and a value of 4 for any response of "very untrue" for both negatively and positively worded statements. This confounded the direction of the responses and, as necessary, the statements are recoded for this study such that a value of 4 is equal to a high internal locus of control and a value of 1 is equal to a high external locus of control.

The original index contained 30 items; however, seven of those items had low response rates ($< 25\%$). These seven items were dropped for the current study. The final 23-item index has high reliability ($\alpha = 0.83$). A factor analysis, using principal components factoring, is used to test whether the remaining 23 items load on one factor. A correlation matrix is produced (Appendix Table 3A) and a factor analysis is conducted (see Table 7).[11] Factor 1 has an eigenvalue of 4.58 and explains 82% of the variance. The remaining factors have eigenvalues below 1.[12] A scree plot (Figure 7) reveals that a one-factor model is sufficient. The locus of control measure is calculated using postestimation regression (i.e., summation of the factor loadings) to generate a predicted factor score. This is a continuous index ranging from -4.891 to 1.342 (mean = -3.93e-10; st. dev. = 0.929) and is slightly right skewed (skew: -0.889).

Typically factor loadings of 0.70 or larger are used to indicate that two variables represent one factor (Raubenheimer, 2004). However, the predicted factor score is used to represent locus of control for this study despite the low factor loadings because this research is exploratory, and the eigenvalues and scree plot indicate that a one-factor model is appropriate.

Table 7. Item wording, descriptive statistics, and factor loadings for each question (N=1,767)

Item Wording of Outcome Expectancy	N	Mean	St. Dev.	Factor Loading
1. Can understand math	1,767	3.183	1.044	0.328
2. Cannot figure out answers in school	1,767	3.457	0.848	0.394
3. Cannot do work expected in school	1,767	3.552	0.767	0.455
4. Can understand what they read	1,767	3.266	0.952	0.449
5. Cannot do well in school	1,767	3.617	0.733	0.477
6. Can finish assignments/homework	1,767	3.551	0.761	0.535

Table 7, continued. Item wording, descriptive statistics, and factor loadings for each question (N=1,767)

Item Wording of Outcome Expectancy	N	Mean	St. Dev.	Factor Loading
7. Can make school better for self	1,767	3.528	0.748	0.596
8. Cannot get parents to listen	1,767	3.183	1.044	0.352
9. Can get parents to do things they like	1,767	3.124	0.949	0.501
10. Can get help from parents	1,767	3.533	0.761	0.560
11. Can talk with parents about bad things	1,767	3.062	1.021	0.520
12. Can be self with parents	1,767	3.132	0.989	0.438
13. Can make things better at home with parents	1,767	3.386	0.854	0.584
14. Have control over own future	1,767	2.923	1.066	0.282
15. Can become successful	1,767	3.673	0.658	0.549
16. Can go far in the world	1,767	3.573	0.748	0.515
17. Cannot make self happy in future	1,767	3.600	0.756	0.399
18. Can do things safely with friends in neighborhood	1,767	3.088	1.001	0.366
19. Cannot avoid gangs in neighborhood	1,767	3.445	0.915	0.409
20. Cannot avoid being scared on way to school	1,767	3.377	0.819	0.380
21. Feel safe alone in neighborhood	1,767	2.889	1.068	0.303
22. Can be safe within a few blocks of home	1,767	3.044	1.048	0.331
23. Cannot avoid fights in neighborhood	1,767	3.101	1.046	0.314

Index reliability coefficient: 0.832

Figure 7. Scree plot of eigenvalues after factor analysis

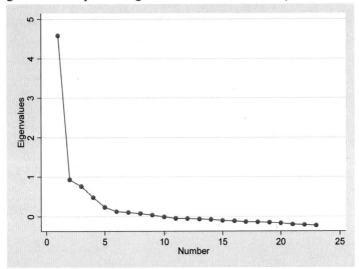

ANOVA is used to determine whether there are differences in locus of control among respondents. There are significant differences in mean locus of control between cohorts ($p < 0.05$) and racial/ethnic groups ($p < 0.000$) suggesting that there may be differences in locus of control orientation related to age and race/ethnicity. There is no difference in mean locus of control between males and females ($p > 0.05$).

As noted earlier, locus of control is assessed at Wave 2; during the same interview that self-reported offending is measured and therefore temporal ordering may be an issue in determining causality. This is not only because data regarding locus of control and offending are gathered at the same time point, but because the questions ask youths about their locus of control without asking about a specific time frame and the questions pertaining to involvement in crime ask about the past 12 months for violence and drug dealing and the past three to six years for trouble with police. For this study, locus of control is measured at Wave 2 because research has demonstrated that locus of control may change over time it is more meaningful to capture locus of control in close proximity to the behavior in question. Further, collective efficacy, neighborhood context, and family context are measured between three and six years before Wave 2 and using Wave 3 self-reported crime data would increase this gap to six to nine years. However, to address the issue of temporal ordering models using Wave 3 self-reported crime as dependent variables are employed and the results are noted in Chapter 4.

In order to address whether the temporal sequencing of locus of control and crime is an issue, chi-square tests were employed to determine if there is stability in locus of control within persons between Wave 2 and Wave 3[13] to complement the chi-square tests conducted for crime (see Table 6). For this test, locus of control at Waves 2 and 3 for 1,004 youths is measured using additive scales for the 23 locus of control items. A higher score indicates a more internal locus of control. The mean of locus of control at Wave 2 is 77.11 (st. dev. = 9.34) and scores ranged from 47 to 92. The mean of locus of control at Wave 3 is 75.93 (st. dev. = 9.65) and scores ranged from 35 to 92. The chi-square tests (using two different sample groupings) indicate a moderate association between locus of control at Wave 2 and Wave 3 (Table 8). There is some change and some stability in individual locus of control scores across these Waves of data collection. Further, locus of control scores at Wave 2 and Wave 3 are positively correlated (0.395).

Table 8. Stability of locus of control between Wave 2 and Wave 3

Number of groups for comparison	χ^2	df	Phi / Cramer's V
Two groups *(Above median; below median)*	76.706***	1	0.276***
Three groups *(25% bottom scores; 50% middle scores; 25% top scores)*	124.776***	4	0.249***

***$p < 0.000$

Collective Efficacy

Collective efficacy in youths' Wave 1 neighborhood is measured using data from the Community Survey (CS). Following Sampson et al. (1997), collective efficacy is measured as the combination of two constructs: informal social control and social cohesion. Informal social control was assessed by asking respondents how likely (responses ranging from very likely to very unlikely) their neighbors could be counted on to "intervene" in the following situations: (i) "children were skipping school and hanging out on a street corner;" (ii) "children were spray-painting graffiti on a local building;" (iii) "children were showing disrespect to an adult;" (iv) a "fight broke out in front of their house;" and (v) "the fire station close to their home was threatened with budget cuts."

Social cohesion was assessed by asking respondents how strongly they agreed (responses ranging from strongly agree to strongly disagree) with the following statements: (i) "people around here are willing to help their neighbors;" (ii) "this is a close-knit neighborhood;" (iii) "people in this neighborhood can be trusted;" (iv) "people in this neighborhood generally don't get along with each other;" and (v) "people in this neighborhood do not share the same values."[14] Sampson et al. (1997) found that informal social control and social cohesion were highly correlated and combined them into one construct labeled collective efficacy.

Maxwell and colleagues (2011) note that the dataset Sampson et al. constructed and that was archived by ICPSR does not contain a single, unifying variable combining informal social control and social cohesion as a measure of collective efficacy. However, Sampson et al. (1997: 924, footnote 21) indicate that the collective efficacy measure was constructed by combining responses to the 5 informal social control and 5 social cohesion items contained in the archive and creating an average score. They used these data to develop a neighborhood-level measure of collective efficacy for each of the 342 NCs. One of the original 343 NCs was removed because it contained O'Hare airport and resulted in an insufficient sample (see Morenoff, 2003). Following this logic, the informal social control and social cohesion variables from the CS were summed and averaged to develop a collective efficacy measure for each of the 80 NCs represented in the LCS data (see Table 9) (see also Maimon and Browning, 2010).

Table 9. Average informal social control, social cohesion, and collective efficacy measures for 80 neighborhood clusters

	N	Mean	St. Dev.	Min	Max
Informal Social Control	80	3.470	0.341	2.643	4.241
Social Cohesion	80	3.375	0.277	2.752	4.171
Collective Efficacy	80	3.423	0.293	2.859	4.182

It is noted that the data on collective efficacy were captured between three and six years before the Wave 2 locus of control and self-reported offending data which were collected between 1997 and 2000. The measure of collective efficacy is only available from the 1994-1995 CS. A second community survey was conducted in 2000. However, the data from that study are not publicly available. While there are pros and cons for using data from an earlier data collection point, an independent macro-level measure of collective efficacy that is gathered from respondents other than the youths in the study is only available from the 1994-1995 CS.[15]

Youths' moving out of a neighborhood cluster between interview waves, which may result in differential exposure to neighborhood collective efficacy, is one factor to consider. However, in the current study, only 18% (N = 319) of the sample moved between Wave 1 and Wave 2, with 88 of the 319 youths moving outside of Chicago. Despite the low correlation (0.247) between neighborhood collective efficacy at Wave 1 and Wave 2 among those who moved from their Wave 1 neighborhood but remained in Chicago (N = 231), collective efficacy is measured at subjects' Wave 1 neighborhood for several reasons. First, by measuring collective efficacy at Wave 1, a temporal ordering between this construct and the dependent variables (i.e., violence, drug dealing, and trouble with police) can be investigated (Duncan and Raudenbush, 1999; Wheaton and Clarke, 2003). This assumes that collective efficacy has a lagged effect on development and behavior that endures over time. Second, neighborhood and family context constructs are measured at Wave 1 and a more comprehensive contextual picture can emerge by examining the influence of all the contextual factors at Wave 1 on the outcomes measured at Wave 2. Finally, the number of subjects nested in each NC would diminish if collective efficacy in subjects' Wave 2 neighborhood was used for this study. In Wave 1, study subjects lived in the 80 original LCS neighborhood clusters, and only 3 of these NCs contained one youth. In Wave 2, however, study subjects lived in 137 NCs, and 76 NCs contained only one youth. Using Wave 2 collective efficacy data would therefore greatly reduce statistical power and ability to detect within neighborhood variability.

One concern with this gap between measurements is that there would be significant changes in levels of collective efficacy during these two time points. While Bursik (1986, 1988) refuted Shaw and McKay's (1942/1969) claim that there is significant stability in neighborhoods, neighborhood changes evolve incrementally and somewhat slowly over time (see Reiss, 1986). Further, Chicago was partially chosen as the PHDCN study site because of the stability of its neighborhoods (Inter-University Consortium for Political and Social Research, Project on Human Development in Chicago Neighborhoods Website, accessed 2009) and Sampson (2006) notes the stability of collective efficacy in neighborhoods over time (but see Sampson and Sharkey, 2008). However, using the PHDCN data Sharkey and Sampson (2010) found that moving within Chicago increased risk of violent offending, exposure to violence, and violent victimization while moving out of Chicago was associated with a decrease in violent offending and exposure to violence.

Contextual Control Variables

The contextual control variables examined in this study are neighborhood context and family context. Appendix Table 4A displays a correlation matrix for locus of control, collective efficacy, neighborhood context, and family context. Some of the neighborhood context and family context variables are similar (e.g., neighborhood level family disruption and individual-level family disruption). However, the CS and LCS samples are independent and the family context variables are not highly correlated with the neighborhood context variables. Therefore, they represent distinct concepts at different levels of measurement.[16]

Neighborhood Context

For this study, indicators of neighborhood context are residential mobility, socioeconomic status, ethnic heterogeneity, and family disruption (see Table 10 for descriptive statistics). Data aggregated by neighborhood clusters (NCs) for these measures are not available in the dataset and were therefore created. Residential mobility, socioeconomic status, and family disruption were estimated for the 80 NCs by collapsing individual responses to questions from the Community Survey's individual-level data file that address the construct of interest and to provide a mean response. Neighborhood ethnic heterogeneity was drawn from the LCS Wave 1 Master File.

Neighborhood level residential mobility was measured by asking CS respondents how many times they moved in the past 5 years. These data were collapsed and an average score was created for each NC. The range is 0.164 to 2.578 (mean = 1.041; st. dev. = 0.525).

Neighborhood level socioeconomic status (SES) was measured using a 3-level variable developed to stratify NC selection for the CS. The low SES category had 27 NCs

(33.75%), the medium SES category had 30 NCs (37.5%), and
the high SES category had 23 NCs (28.75%).

Table 10. Neighborhood level context variable descriptive
         statistics

	N	Mean	St. Dev.	Min	Max
Residential Mobility	80	1.041	0.525	0.164	2.578
Socioeconomic Status	80	1.950	0.794	1	3
Ethnic Heterogeneity	80	3.762	2.136	1	7
Family Disruption	80	0.173	0.084	0	0.390

Ethnic heterogeneity is not available in the CS data due to
data limitations of the restricted user's agreement with ICPSR[17]
and therefore each NC's ethnic heterogeneity was measured
using Wave 1 LCS data (see Table 1). NCs were stratified using
seven racial/ethnic categories: $\geq$ 70% African American (N = 17;
21.25%), $\geq$ 70% White (N = 12; 15%), $\geq$ 70% Hispanic (N = 8;
10%), $\geq$ 20% Hispanic and $\geq$ 20% White (N = 13; 16.25%), $\geq$
20% Hispanic and $\geq$ 20% African American (N = 8; 10%), $\geq$
20% African American and $\geq$ 20% White (N = 10; 12.5%), and
Other (N = 12; 15%).

Family disruption was measured using CS respondents
current marital status. Responses included single, separated,
divorced, married, widowed, and live with partner.
Neighborhood-level family disruption was recorded as a binary
variable (0 = no/1 = yes) and was operationalized as the average
number of CS respondents reporting that they were separated or
divorced. The data were collapsed and averaged to provide a
mean score for each NC (mean = 0.173; st. dev. = 0.084; range 0
to 0.390).

Family Context
Family context was measured as the youths' primary caregiver's
immigrant status, socioeconomic status (SES), family disruption,
family size, and parental monitoring (see Table 11 for descriptive

statistics). This information is captured at the individual respondent level and was obtained from the Wave 1 LCS.

Table 11. Family context variable descriptive statistics

	N	Mean	St. Dev.	Min	Max
Immigrant Status	1,767	0.41	0.49	0	1
SES	1,753	-0.11	1.42	-3.16	3.52
Family Disruption	1,744	0.16	0.37	0	1
Family Size	1,725	5.35	2.01	2	14
Parental Monitoring	1,600	21.30	2.53	6	24

Primary caregiver's immigrant status was calculated by converting the question "When did you come to live in the U.S.?" to a binary variable. Observations without a year recorded were coded as 0 and observations with a year were coded as 1.[18] This provides a no/yes response for determining whether a youth's primary caregiver immigrated to the United States. This recoding does not provide length of time living in the U.S. which may influence acculturation, country of origin, or whether they immigrated legally or illegally. Almost 41% of the primary caregivers in the study sample were immigrants (st. dev. = 0.491).

Family socioeconomic status is a composite measure developed by the PHDCN scientific group and contains primary caregiver's maximum education level, salary, and description of most recent job. The average principal components measure of family socioeconomic status is -0.108.

Family disruption was operationalized as the subject's primary caregiver's marital status being separated or divorced. Other marital status options were single, married, widowed, and living with partner. Family disruption is a dichotomous variable with 1 indicating separated/divorced (N = 281; 16.11%) and 0 indicating all other categories (N = 1,463; 83.89%).

Family size is measured as number of persons living in the household (excluding the youth). Interviewers asked the primary caregiver for each household resident's relationship to the youth, and allowed for up to 17 possible responses. The family size variable used in this study was created by recoding the responses as a binary variable (0 = no response/1 = response) and summing to determine number of persons residing in the household with the youth. Family size ranged from 2 to 14 (mean = 5.347; st. dev. = 2.005).

Parental monitoring is measured using a validated 24-item scale (Appendix Table 5A; $\alpha = 0.67$) developed by Caldwell and Bradley (1984) (see also Bradley et al., 2000; Browning, Leventhal, and Brooks-Gunn, 2004). Primary caregivers of the youths were asked about rules and discipline techniques as well as their youth's schedule. Responses to the 24-items were binary (0 = no/yes = 1) and the questions are worded as such that a "yes" response indicated greater supervision than a "no" response. An additive scale was created using the responses to this instrument. Scores ranged from 6 to 24 and was left skewed with the majority of scores indicating higher levels of monitoring (mean = 21.27; st. dev. = 2.531).

Individual-Level Control Variables

The individual-level control variables used in this study are youth's age/cohort, sex, and race/ethnicity (see Table 12 for descriptive statistics). These demographic variables were taken from the LCS Wave 2 Master File. The study subjects' ages at Wave 2 ranged from 9 to 19. Youths in Cohorts 9, 12, and 15 were 9 – 13, 12 – 17, and 15 – 19 years old, respectively. The subject's actual age at the time of the Wave 2 interview is recorded (e.g., 12.33 years); it is not rounded and is therefore a continuous variable. Youth's cohort membership is a categorical variable. A binary variable was created for each of the three cohorts to provide a reference group. Approximately 35% of the youth are in Cohort 9, 35% are in Cohort 12, and 30% are in Cohort 15. Youth's sex is included as a dichotomous variable (0 = female/1 = male). The sample is split almost evenly between percentage of females (49.63%) and males (50.37%).

Race/ethnicity was measured as a categorical variable. The majority of subjects were Hispanic (N = 728; 42.18%) or African American (N = 535; 31.00%). Whites comprised 14.66% of the study sample (N = 253), and 12.17% were classified as Asian, Pacific Islander, Native American, or Other (N = 210).

Table 12. Individual-level control variable descriptive statistics

	N	%	Mean	St. Dev.	Min	Max
Age/Cohort						
Age	1,767	100.00	14.025	2.479	9.109	19.890
Cohort 9	694	34.91			0	1
Cohort 12	701	35.26			0	1
Cohort 15	593	29.83			0	1
Sex						
Male	890	46.63			1	1
Female	877	50.37			0	0
Race/Ethnicity						
African American	535	31.00			0	1
Hispanic	728	42.18			0	1
White/Other	436	26.82			0	1

Bivariate Relationships between Dependent and Individual-Level Variables

In this section, the bivariate relationships between the three dependent variables (violence, drug dealing, and trouble with police) and locus of control, family context and the individual-level control variables are examined. Bivariate analyses establish the relationship between the dependent variables and individual-level variables without taking into account the potential influence of neighborhood context. The bivariate relationships are derived using negative binomial and logit regression models. A separate model is employed for each independent variable to determine its relationship with each dependent variable.

The violence and drug dealing scales are right-skewed and follow a Poisson distribution. There is evidence of over-dispersion in these dependent variables because the variances (1.655 and 0.069) are larger than the means (0.638 and 0.047) for both the violence and drug dealing scales, respectively. Likelihood ratio tests also provide significant evidence of over-dispersion for the violence scale (786.91; $p < 0.000$) and drug dealing scale (60.24; $p < 0.000$). In cases of over-dispersion, a Poisson model underfits the data (Long and Freese, 2006). Over-dispersion results in consistent but inefficient estimates and the standard errors are biased downward which affects hypothesis tests. Since the assumptions of Poisson are violated in the violence and drug dealing scales, bivariate relationships for these outcomes were derived using negative binomial regression models. The negative binomial probability distribution is

$$P(Y_i = y_i) = \frac{\Gamma(y_i + \phi)}{y_i \Gamma(\phi)} \frac{\phi^{\phi} \lambda_i^{y_i}}{(\phi + \lambda_i)^{\phi - y_i}} 1$$

where Γ is the gamma function and ϕ is the reciprocal residual variance.

Trouble with police is a binary measure indicating whether subjects had contact with police since the Wave 1 interview (0 = no/1 = yes). Bivariate relationships between the trouble with police dependent variable and individual-level variables were derived using logistic regression models. The logit link is

$$\eta_{ij} = \log\left(\frac{\varphi_{ij}}{1 - \varphi_{ij}}\right)$$

where η_{ij} represents the log of the odds of being in trouble with police since the Wave 1 interview and φ_{ij} represents the probability of a youth being in trouble with police since the Wave 1 interview.

The results from the bivariate regression models are presented and discussed below. In sum, the bivariate relationships indicate a negative relationship between the outcome variables and main independent variable (locus of control). Table 13 presents the results of the bivariate models.

Violence Scale

Several variables are significantly related to involvement in violence in the past 12 months. The results indicate that youths with a more internal locus of control report less violence (β = -0.346; p < 0.000) than youths reporting a more external locus of control. For each unit increase toward an internal locus of control expected involvement in violence decreases by 0.71 and involvement in violence is expected to decrease by 27.49% for each standard deviation change in locus of control.[19]

For family context variables, youths with a primary caregiver who is a first generation immigrant (β = -0.537; p < 0.000) and youths who receive more parental monitoring (β = -0.054; p < 0.01) are less likely to engage in violence. Compared to youths whose primary caregiver was born in the United States, having a primary caregiver who is a first generation immigrant decreases youths expected involvement in violence by a factor of 0.58. Having a primary caregiver who is a first generation immigrant is expected to decrease involvement in violence by 41.55%. For each unit increase in parental monitoring, involvement in violence is expected to decrease by a factor of 0.95. Involvement in violence is expected to decrease by 19.35% for each standard deviation change in parental monitoring. Family SES, family disruption (i.e., primary caregiver being divorced/separated), and family size are not related to violence.

All of the individual-level control variables are significantly related to involvement in violence. Membership in Cohort 9 (i.e., being younger) (β = -1.044; p < 0.000) and Hispanic (β = -0.481; p < 0.000) are negatively related to violence. Youths who are in Cohort 9 (compared to being in Cohort 12 or 15) or Hispanic (compared to other race/ethnicities) decreases the expected involvement in violence by a factor of 0.35 and 0.62, respectively. Being in Cohort 9 decreases expected involvement in violence by 64.79%, while being Hispanic decreases involvement in violence by 38.18%.

The other individual-level control variables are related to a positive and significant increase in violence. Youths who are African American ($\beta = 0.605$; $p < 0.000$) or male ($\beta = 0.479$; $p < 0.000$) are more likely to be involved in violence than youths of other races/ethnicities or females. Belonging to Cohort 12 ($\beta = 0.236$; $p < 0.05$) or Cohort 15 ($\beta = 0.581$; $p < 0.000$) is positively related to involvement in violence when each are independently compared to youths in the other cohorts. Youths who are African American or male are expected to have an increased involvement in violence over other races/ethnicities and females by a factor of 1.83 and 1.61, respectively. In terms of percent change, being African American increases expected involvement in violence by 83.12% and being male increases expected involvement in violence by 61.44%. Finally, belonging to Cohort 12 or 15 increases expected involvement in violence by a factor of 1.27 and 1.79, respectively. Compared to youths in other cohorts, being in Cohort 12 increases expected involvement in violence by 26.62%, while those in Cohort 15 have an increase of 78.78% in expected violence.

Drug Dealing Scale

Table 13 also shows that several variables are significantly related to drug dealing in the past 12 months. The results indicate that youths who have higher levels of internal locus of control engage in less drug dealing ($\beta = -0.569$; $p < 0.000$) than youths with higher levels of external locus of control. For each unit increase in internal locus of control expected involvement in drug dealing decreases by 0.57, and involvement in drug dealing is expected to decrease by 41.05% for each standard deviation increase in internal locus of control.[20]

For family context variables, youths with a primary caregiver who is a first generation immigrant ($\beta = -0.768$; $p < 0.05$) are less likely to engage in drug dealing than youths whose primary caregiver is a native born United States citizen.

Table 13. Bivariate relationship between dependent and individual-level variables

Variable	Violence Scale			Drug Dealing Scale			Trouble With Police		
	b	SE	Factor Change	b	SE	Factor Change	b	SE	Odds Ratio
Locus of Control	-0.346***	0.053	0.707	-0.569***	0.122	0.566	-0.439***	0.069	0.645
Family Context									
Immigrant	-0.537***	0.103	0.584	-0.768*	0.304	0.464	-0.536***	0.149	0.585
SES	-0.038	0.036	0.963	-0.031	0.097	0.969	-0.034	0.049	0.966
Family Disruption	0.029	0.136	1.029	0.309	0.357	1.362	0.366*	0.174	1.442
Family Size	-0.005	0.023	0.995	-0.102	0.069	0.903	0.042	0.033	1.043
Parental Monitoring	-0.054**	0.021	0.947	-0.174***	0.049	0.840	-0.112***	0.025	0.894
Control Variables									
Cohort 9	-1.044***	0.113	0.352	-3.764***	1.016	0.023	-1.512***	0.205	0.220
Cohort 12	0.236*	0.103	1.266	-0.651*	0.311	0.521	-0.129	0.146	0.879
Cohort 15	0.581***	0.104	1.788	2.030***	0.286	7.614	1.258***	0.142	3.518
Male	0.479***	0.099	1.614	0.554*	0.281	1.740	0.761***	0.145	2.140
African American	0.605***	0.104	1.831	0.269	0.291	1.309	0.459**	0.144	1.582
Hispanic	-0.481***	0.104	0.618	-0.799**	0.303	0.449	-0.486**	0.148	0.615

* $p < 0.05$ ** $p < 0.01$ *** $p < 0.000$

Youths who experience more parental monitoring (β = -0.174; p < 0.000) are less likely to report selling drugs in the past 12 months than youths with less parental monitoring. Having a primary caregiver who is a first generation immigrant decreases youths expected involvement in drug dealing by a factor of 0.46 and for each unit increase in parental monitoring, involvement in drug dealing is expected to decrease by a factor of 0.84. In terms of percent change, having a primary caregiver who is a first generation immigrant decreases expected involvement in drug dealing by 53.60% relative to youths whose primary caregiver was born in the United States. For each standard deviation change in parental monitoring, expected involvement in drug dealing decreases by 35.61%. Family SES, family disruption, and family size are not related to youths' involvement in drug dealing.

Most of the individual-level control variables are significantly related to involvement in drug dealing. Membership in Cohort 9 (β = -3.764; p < 0.000) or Cohort 12 (β = -0.651; p < 0.05), or being Hispanic (β = -0.799; p < 0.01) are all negatively related to drug dealing. Youths' in Cohort 9 or Cohort 12, or who are Hispanic, have a decreased expected involvement in drug dealing over youths in Cohort 15 and those who are not Hispanic by a factor of 0.02, 0.52, and 0.45, respectively. Compared to other Cohorts, being in Cohort 9 or Cohort 12 decreases the expected involvement in drug dealing by 97.68% or 47.85%, respectively. Relative to other races/ethnicities, being Hispanic decreases the expected involvement in drug dealing by 55.02%. African American is not related to expected involvement in drug dealing.

Other individual-level control variables are related to a positive and significant increase in drug dealing. Youths who are male (β = 0.554; p < 0.05) are more likely to engage in drug dealing than youths who are female. Being male (as opposed to female) increases expected involvement in drug dealing by a factor of 1.74, and increases expected involvement in drug dealing by 74.02%. Finally, compared to other cohorts, belonging to Cohort 15 ($\beta = 2.030$; $p < 0.000$) is also positively related to drug dealing. Compared to Cohorts 9 and 12, membership in Cohort 15 increases expected involvement in drug dealing by a factor of 7.61, and increases expected involvement in drug dealing by 661.41%.

Trouble with Police

Results (Table 13) indicate that several variables are significantly related to being in trouble with the police since the Wave 1 interview. Youths with higher levels of internal locus of control are less likely to be in trouble with the police ($\beta = -0.439$; $p < 0.000$). For each unit increase in internal locus of control the odds of being in trouble with police decreases by 0.64, and trouble with police is expected to decrease by 33.49% for each standard deviation change in internal locus of control.[21]

For family context variables, youths who have a primary caregiver who is a first generation immigrant ($\beta = -0.536$; $p < 0.000$) and those who experience more parental monitoring ($\beta = -0.112$; $p < 0.000$) are less likely to be in trouble with the police. Compared to having a primary caregiver who was born in the United States, having a primary caregiver who is a first generation immigrant decreases the odds of being in trouble with the police by 0.58. In terms of percent change, having a primary caregiver who is a first generation immigrant decreases expected trouble with police by 41.49%. Increased levels of parental monitoring are related to a decrease in the odds of youths being in trouble with the police by 0.89. For each standard deviation change in parental monitoring, expected trouble with the police decreases by 24.67%.

On the other hand, experiencing family disruption (i.e., having a primary caregiver who is separated/divorced) increases the odds of being in trouble with the police by 1.44 ($\beta = 0.366$; $p < 0.05$). Expected trouble with police is 44.19% higher among youths whose primary caregiver is separated or divorced compared to youths who do not experience family disruption. Family SES and family size are not related to trouble with the police.

Most of the individual-level control variables are significantly related to being in trouble with the police. Membership in Cohort 9 ($\beta = -1.512$; $p < 0.000$) and Hispanic ethnicity ($\beta = -0.486$; $p < 0.01$) are negatively related to trouble with police and decrease the odds of being in trouble with the police by 0.22 and 0.61, respectively. Belonging to Cohort 9 decreases expected trouble with police by 77.95% compared to youths in other cohorts. Expected trouble with the police is 38.49% lower among Hispanic youth. Compared to other cohorts, belonging to Cohort 12 is negatively related to trouble with police, but is not statistically significant.

The other individual-level control variables are positively and significantly related to trouble with the police. Youths who are African American ($\beta = 0.459$; $p < 0.01$) or male ($\beta = 0.761$; $p < 0.000$) are more likely to be in trouble with the police than youths who are non-African American or female. Compared to other cohorts, membership in Cohort 15 ($\beta = 1.258$; $p < 0.000$) is positively related to trouble with police. Being African American, being male, or in Cohort 15, increases the odds of being in trouble with police by 1.58, 2.14, and 3.52, respectively. Being African American (as opposed to other races/ethnicities) and male (as opposed to female) are related to a 58.25% and 114.04% increase in expected trouble with police, respectively. Compared to youths in other cohorts, being in Cohort 15 increases expected trouble with police by 251.84%.

ANALYTIC APPROACH AND MODELS

This study uses data on 1,767 youths nested in 80 neighborhood clusters (NCs) which necessitates the exploration of multilevel modeling. One statistical method for analyzing multilevel, nested data is hierarchical linear modeling (HLM). The practical utility of this method is aptly stated by Raudenbush and Bryk (2002: 6-7), "With hierarchical linear models, each of the levels in this structure is formally represented by its own submodel. These submodels express relationships among variables within a given level, and specify how variables at one level influence relations occurring at another." Multilevel modeling allows for the estimation of variance between individuals within the same NC, and variance between NCs. Further, it allows for the estimation of effects at each level and across levels.

Multilevel modeling accounts for similarities in standard errors since observations may not be independent – individuals will likely share some characteristics with others who live in their NC. These correlated error terms violate the assumptions of ordinary least squares regression. To accommodate this lack of independence, HLM includes an error term for level-2 data (Raudenbush and Bryk, 2002).

For the analyses, two study data sets were created: one each for individual-level and neighborhood level data. The CS and LCS data share a common variable, neighborhood cluster, for data linking purposes and this variable appears in both study data sets. Individual-level data are fitted to a regression equation at level-1. The level-1 model estimates individual-level outcomes. Neighborhood level data are fitted to a regression equation at level-2. Level-2 data provides information on whether individual-level variables differ by neighborhood context. The models examined in this study are described in the next section.

It is anticipated that multilevel models will be appropriate for answering the research questions examined in this study due the nested nature of the data. To test this assumption, I run a series of one-way ANOVA with random effects baseline models (e.g., unconditional or null models) and calculate intra-class correlation coefficients (ICC). The unconditional (null) mixed-effects model is

$$\eta_{ij} = \gamma_{00} + u_{01} + r_{ij}$$

and the ICC equation is

$$\rho = \frac{\sigma_{u0}^2}{(\sigma_{u0}^2 + \sigma_r^2)}$$

where

ρ = intraclass correlation; which measures variance in the outcome explained by the level-2 units

σ_{u0}^{2} = *between group variability; level-2 variance*

σ_{r}^{2} = *within group variability; level-1 variance.*

The ICC measures the proportion of variance in the dependent variable accounted for by the level-2 variables (e.g., collective efficacy). The equation divides the level-2 variance by the sum of the level-1 variance and level-2 variance to arrive at the ICC. A higher ICC indicates that the level-2 variables explain some of the variance in the dependent variable and that multilevel methods should be used.

After these diagnostics are conducted, and assuming multilevel models are indeed appropriate, hierarchical linear models will be employed to address the research questions.[22] In multilevel modeling, the systems of equations models (depicting the level-1 and level-2 equations separately), mixed-effects models (depicting an equation combining the level-1 and level-2 models), or both can be used to demonstrate the multilevel model (Luke, 2004). Here, only the mixed-effects models are shown to demonstrate the relationship between variables at both levels.

Research question 1: Does locus of control influence self-reported involvement in crime?

The first research question is separated into four subquestions and models. Model 1a is a random-intercept model and addresses whether there is a relationship between locus of control and each of the crime outcomes, regardless of neighborhood. To answer this question, locus of control is entered into the models uncentered and the intercept and slope error terms are fixed. By not centering the independent variable, the intercept is equal to the expected value of Y_{ij} when X_{ij} is zero and the overall influence of locus of control on involvement in violence, drug dealing, and trouble with police can be determined. For this model the error terms are fixed because the focus is on the overall influence of locus of control on various measures of crime. This means that, for this model, it is assumed that crime and locus of control do not differ across neighborhoods.[23] This model does not contain any level-2 predictors.

The mixed-effects models are:

violence scale (past 12 months)$_{ij}$ = γ_{00} + γ_{10} (locus of control at Wave 2$_{ij}$) + r$_{ij}$

drug dealing scale (past 12 months)$_{ij}$ = γ_{00} + γ_{10} (locus of control at Wave 2$_{ij}$) + r$_{ij}$

trouble with police (since Wave 1)$_{ij}$ = γ_{00} + γ_{10} (locus of control at Wave 2$_{ij}$)[24]

To address whether the relationship between locus of control and crime varies by neighborhood, a second set of models are employed. Model 1b is a random coefficients regression model and the intercepts and slopes in level-1 are allowed to vary across level-2 neighborhoods. Locus of control is entered into the models group-mean centered and the error terms were allowed to vary. Group-mean centering the independent variable accounts for contextual effects. In more simple terms, these models will indicate whether there is variation in the key independent variable, locus of control, across neighborhoods by centering on the average of the group within a neighborhood. Therefore, the error terms are freed and allowed to vary to test whether the intercept and the average influence of locus of control on crime vary by neighborhood. This model does not contain any level-2 predictors. The mixed-effects models are:

violence scale (past 12 months)$_{ij}$ = γ_{00} + γ_{10} (locus of control at Wave 2$_{ij}$)+ u_0 + u_1(locus of control at Wave 2$_{ij}$) + r_{ij}

drug dealing scale (past 12 months)$_{ij}$ = γ_{00} + γ_{10} (locus of control at Wave 2$_{ij}$)+ u_o + u_1(locus of control at Wave 2$_{ij}$) + r_{ij}

trouble with police (since Wave 1)$_{ij}$ = γ_{00} + γ_{10} (locus of control at Wave 2$_{ij}$)+ u_0 + u_1(locus of control at Wave 2$_{ij}$)

Additional models are employed to examine the influence of potential individual and contextual variables. Model 1c controls for individual-level variables and Model 1d controls for individual-level, neighborhood context, and family context variables.

Model 1c is a random coefficients regression model where only the level-1 intercept is allowed to vary. Locus of control is group-mean centered and the other variables are entered into the model uncentered. The mixed-effects models for Model 1c are:

violence scale (past 12 months)$_{ij}$ = γ_{00} + γ_{10}(locus of control$_{ij}$) +γ_{20}(cohort 12$_{ij}$) + γ_{30}(cohort 15$_{ij}$) + γ_{40}(male$_{ij}$) + γ_{50}(African American$_{ij}$) + γ_{60}(Hispanic$_{ij}$) + u_{0j} + r_{ij}

drug dealing scale (past 12 months)$_{ij}$ = γ_{00} + γ_{10}(locus of control$_{ij}$) +γ_{20}(cohort 12$_{ij}$) + γ_{30}(cohort 15$_{ij}$) + γ_{40}(male$_{ij}$) + γ_{50}(African American$_{ij}$) + γ_{60}(Hispanic$_{ij}$) + u_{0j} + r_{ij}

trouble with police (since Wave 1)$_{ij}$ = γ_{00} + γ_{10}(locus of control$_{ij}$) +γ_{20}(cohort 12$_{ij}$) + γ_{30}(cohort 15$_{ij}$) + γ_{40}(male$_{ij}$) + γ_{50}(African American$_{ij}$) + γ_{60}(Hispanic$_{ij}$) + u_0

Model 1d is also a random coefficients regression model. In this model, locus of control and family SES are group-mean centered. Neighborhood context variables residential mobility, SES, and ethnic heterogeneity are grand-mean centered.[25] All other variables are entered in to the model at their natural metrics. Only one model is shown below since the level-1 model and level-2 model for a count outcome (i.e., violence scale, drug dealing scale) are the same as the level-1 and level-2 models for a binary outcome (i.e., trouble with police) (Raudenbush and Bryk, 2002: 295-296 and 310). The mixed-effects model for Model 1d is:

violence scale (past 12 months)$_{ij}$ = γ_{00} + γ_{01}(neighborhood residential mobility$_j$) + γ_{02}(neighborhood SES$_j$) + γ_{03}(neighborhood ethnic heterogeneity$_j$) + γ_{04}(neighborhood family disruption$_j$) + γ_{10}(locus of control$_{ij}$) + γ_{20}(immigrant status$_{ij}$) + γ_{30}(family SES$_{ij}$) + γ_{40}(family disruption$_{ij}$) + γ_{50}(family size$_{ij}$) + γ_{60}(parental monitoring$_{ij}$) + γ_{70}(cohort 12$_{ij}$) + γ_{80}(cohort 15$_{ij}$) + γ_{90}(male$_{ij}$) + γ_{100}(African American$_{ij}$) + γ_{110}(Hispanic$_{ij}$) + u_{0j} + r_{ij}

Research question 2: Does collective efficacy influence self-reported involvement in crime?

The second research question examines the influence of collective efficacy on youths' involvement in crime. Model 2a employs a means-as-outcomes regression model where the emphasis is on the level-2 predictor collective efficacy. Collective efficacy is not centered in order to retain variability across neighborhoods. The intercept error term is fixed and is assumed to not vary randomly across neighborhoods. The mixed-effects models are:

violence scale (past 12 months)$_{ij}$ = γ_{00} + γ_{01} (collective efficacy at Wave 1$_j$) + r_{ij}

drug dealing scale (past 12 months)$_{ij}$ = γ_{00} + γ_{01} (collective efficacy at Wave 1$_j$) + r_{ij}

trouble with police (since Wave 1)$_{ij}$ = γ_{00} + γ_{01} (collective efficacy at Wave 1$_j$)

Model 2b employs a means-as-outcomes model and examines the relationship between collective efficacy and crime while controlling for neighborhood context and family context. In this model the intercept variance is allowed to vary while the error terms for family context variables are fixed. Neighborhood context variables residential mobility, SES, and ethnic heterogeneity are grand-mean centered. Family context variables family SES and parental monitoring are group-mean centered. All other variables are entered into the model at their natural metrics. The mixed-effects model is:[26]

violence scale (past 12 months)$_{ij}$ = γ_{00} + γ_{01}(collective efficacy at Wave 1$_j$) +γ_{02}(neighborhood residential mobility$_j$) + γ_{03}(neighborhood SES$_j$) + γ_{04}(neighborhood ethnic heterogeneity$_j$) + γ_{05}(neighborhood family disruption$_j$) + γ_{10}(immigrant status$_{ij}$) + γ_{20}(family SES$_{ij}$) + γ_{30}(family disruption$_{ij}$) + γ_{40}(family size$_{ij}$) + γ_{50}(parental monitoring$_{ij}$) + u_{0j} + r_{ij}

Research question 3: Does collective efficacy moderate the relationship between locus of control and self-reported involvement in crime?

Model 3a examines the relationship between collective efficacy, locus of control, and crime by including locus of control at level-1 and collective efficacy at level-2. This model is an extension of a random-effects ANCOVA model and adds a level-2 covariate. In this model, locus of control is group-mean centered and its error term is fixed. The error term for the level-2 covariate is allowed to vary. The mixed-models are:

violence scale (past 12 months)$_{ij}$ = γ_{00} + γ_{01}(collective efficacy at Wave 1$_j$) + γ_{10} (locus of control at Wave 2$_{ij}$) + u_{0j} + r_{ij}

drug dealing scale (past 12 months)$_{ij}$ = γ_{00} + γ_{01}(collective efficacy at Wave 1$_j$) + γ_{10} (locus of control at Wave 2$_{ij}$) + u_{0j} + r_{ij}

trouble with police (since Wave 1)$_{ij}$ = γ_{00} + γ_{01}(collective efficacy at Wave 1$_j$) + γ_{10} (locus of control at Wave 2$_{ij}$) + u_{0j}

In Model 3b, intercepts- and slopes-as-outcomes models are employed to examine whether collective efficacy moderates the relationship between crime and locus of control. Here the level-1 intercept and slopes are modeled using the level-2 predictor collective efficacy. These models result in a cross-level interaction term (collective efficacy x locus of control) by modeling the level-1 slope for locus of control using collective efficacy. Locus of control is group-mean centered and collective efficacy is entered into the model uncentered. The error term for locus of control is fixed and freed for collective efficacy. The mixed-effects models are:

*violence scale (past 12 months)$_{ij}$ = γ_{00} + γ_{01}(collective efficacy at Wave 1$_j$)+ γ_{10} (locus of control at Wave 2$_{ij}$) + γ_{11}(collective efficacy at Wave 1$_j$ * locus of control at Wave 2$_{ij}$) + u_{0j} + r_{ij}*

*drug dealing scale (past 12 months)$_{ij}$ = γ_{00} + γ_{01}(collective efficacy at Wave 1 $_j$) + γ_{10} (locus of control at Wave 2$_{ij}$) + γ_{11}(collective efficacy at Wave 1$_j$ * locus of control at Wave 2$_{ij}$) + u_{0j} + r_{ij}*

*trouble with police (since Wave 1)$_{ij}$ = γ_{00} + γ_{01}(collective efficacy at Wave 1 $_j$) + γ_{10} (locus of control at Wave 2$_{ij}$) + γ_{11}(collective efficacy at Wave 1$_j$ * locus of control at Wave 2$_{ij}$) + u_{0j}*

Model 3c builds on the previous model by adding neighborhood context, family context, and individual-level control variables. In this model the intercept variance is allowed to vary while the error terms for locus of control, the family context variables, and the individual-level control variables are fixed. Locus of control and the family context variable family SES are group-mean centered. Neighborhood context variables residential mobility, SES, and ethnic heterogeneity are grand-mean centered. All other variables are entered into the model at their natural metrics. The mixed-effects model for the violence scale is:[27]

violence scale (past 12 months)$_{ij}$ = γ_{00} + γ_{01}(collective efficacy at Wave 1$_j$) + γ_{02}(neighborhood residential mobility$_j$) + γ_{03}(neighborhood SES$_j$) + γ_{04}(neighborhood ethnic heterogeneity$_j$) + γ_{05}(neighborhood family disruption$_j$) + γ_{10}(locus of control at Wave 2$_{ij}$) + γ_{20}(collective efficacy at Wave 1$_j$ * locus of control at Wave 2$_{ij}$) + γ_{30}(immigrant status$_{ij}$) + γ_{40}(family SES$_{ij}$) + γ_{50}(family disruption$_{ij}$) + γ_{60}(family size$_{ij}$) + γ_{70}(parental monitoring$_{ij}$) + γ_{80} (cohort 12$_{ij}$) + γ_{90}(cohort 15$_{ij}$) + γ_{100}(male$_{ij}$) + γ_{110}(African American$_{ij}$) + γ_{120}(Hispanic$_{ij}$) + u_{0j} + r_{ij}

In this chapter the data used in this study were outlined, univariate statistics and bivariate relationships were examined, and the research questions and models for testing those questions were presented. In the next chapter, the results from these models will be displayed and interpreted.

CHAPTER FOUR

Locus of Control, Collective Efficacy, and Crime

APPROPRIATENESS OF MULTILEVEL MODELS

It is anticipated that multilevel models will be appropriate due to the nested nature of the data. Luke (2004) suggests three types of criteria for determining whether multilevel models are appropriate – namely, statistical, theoretical, and empirical justifications. Each criterion type is discussed in turn below.

There is sufficient statistical rationale for employing multilevel models in this study. The youths are nested in 80 Chicago neighborhoods and it is anticipated that there will be similarities between individuals who reside in the same neighborhood due to clustering. This clustering will likely violate the assumptions of ordinary least squares regression (OLS) that errors are independent, normally distributed, and have a constant variance. Multilevel modeling controls for the clustering of observations within level-2 variables (in this case, urban neighborhoods).

A second method suggested by Luke (2004) is to base methodological decisions on theoretical grounds. Involvement in violence and drug dealing, as well as being in trouble with the police, are expected to vary across neighborhoods. It is believed that neighborhood characteristics will influence youths' behavior. Further, offending behavior is likely to vary within neighborhoods. Therefore, using multilevel modeling techniques will allow for these assumptions to be tested.

A final method suggested by Luke (2004) for determining the appropriateness of using multilevel methods is to base the decision on empirical justification. One method is to visually show the variation between neighborhoods using illustrative graphs. Figures 8-10 depict the variation in the dependent variables by showing the mean involvement in the outcome behavior for each neighborhood.[1]

A more formal and sophisticated empirical justification for the use of multilevel models is to calculate intraclass correlations (ICCs). ICCs determine the proportion of variance in the outcomes explained by the level-2 variables. ICCs greater than zero indicate that neighborhood differences explain at least some of the variance. Fully unconditional (null) models are employed to obtain the variance components necessary to calculate the ICC for each dependent variable.

Figure 8. Violence scale (mean) for each neighborhood

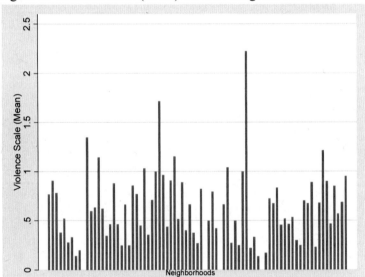

Figure 9. Drug dealing scale (mean) for each neighborhood

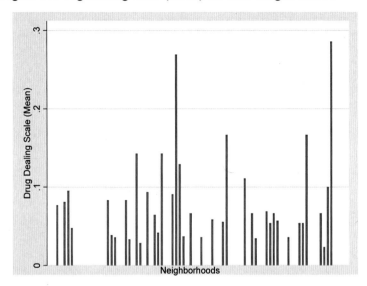

Figure 10. Trouble with police (mean) for each neighborhood

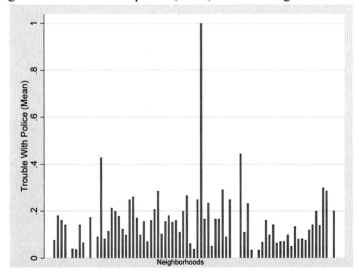

Unconditional (Null) Models

One-way ANOVA with random effects models provide information pertaining to the variation between neighborhoods and the three dependent variables. A fully unconditional, or null, model is constructed for each dependent variable.

The unconditional mixed-effects model for the violence scale is:

$$\textit{violence scale (past 12 months)}_{ij} = \gamma_{00} + u_{0j} + r_{ij}$$

The *violence scale* variable is a youth's score on the violence scale where the potential range of scores is 0 to 12, and the actual range is 0 to 9. The violence scale is an additive scale of 12 items that ask youths whether they have been involved in a series of violent acts in the past 12 months. The fixed effect, γ_{00}, represents the grand mean across all youths. The two error components represent the variability between neighborhoods (u_{0j}) and the variability between youths (r_{ij}).

The unconditional mixed-effects model for the drug dealing scale is:

$$\textit{drug dealing scale (past 12 months)}_{ij} = \gamma_{00} + u_{0j} + r_{ij}$$

In this model, *drug dealing scale* is a youth's score on the drug dealing scale, where the (potential and actual) range is 0 to 3. The drug dealing scale is an additive scale of 3 items which ask youths whether they have engaged in dealing three drugs (marijuana, crack/cocaine, and heroin) in the past 12 months. The fixed effect, γ_{00}, represents the grand mean across all youths. The two error components represent the variability between neighborhoods (u_{0j}) and the variability between youths (r_{ij}).

The unconditional mixed-effects model for the binary outcome trouble with police is:

$$\textit{trouble with police (since Wave 1)}_{ij} = \gamma_{00} + u_{0j}$$

In this model, *trouble with police* is a youth's expected odds of being in trouble with the police since the Wave 1 interview. The fixed effect, γ_{00}, represents the expected odds across all youths. The error component represents the variability between neighborhoods (u_{0j}).

Intraclass Correlations

After the one-way ANOVA with random effects models were fitted to the data, ICCs were calculated by using the variance components from those models. ICCs are more appropriate for continuous outcomes. However, quasi-ICCs are calculated here for the nonlinear models as an added justification for multilevel modeling. In binary outcomes the variance equals the mean and therefore a level-1 variance component is not generated for null models. Following Snijders and Bosker (1999: 223), the level-1 variance is calculated as $\pi^2/3$.

The ICCs indicate that a proportion of the variance in each of the dependent variables is accounted for by neighborhood. According to the ICCs, 4.1% (violence scale), 23.0% (drug dealing scale), and 1.6% (trouble with police) of the variance in these variables is attributed to neighborhood level differences. The percentage of variance explained, and the statistical and theoretical justifications, taken in combination suggest that multilevel models are indeed appropriate. The following sections outline the research questions, models employed to address these questions, and findings. The results reported are from the population-average models with robust standard errors.

RESEARCH QUESTION 1: DOES LOCUS OF CONTROL INFLUENCE SELF-REPORTED INVOLVEMENT IN CRIME?

Model 1a: Influence of Locus of Control on Crime

Model 1a examines the influence of locus of control on crime, regardless of neighborhood. Table 14 displays the results from this model. According to the intercept coefficients expected involvement in violence decreases by 0.50 ($p < 0.000$), expected involvement in drug dealing decreases by 3.28 ($p < 0.000$), and being in trouble with police decreases by 1.89 ($p < 0.000$).[2]

Each unit increase in locus of control decreases expected involvement in violence and drug dealing in the past 12 months by a factor of 0.72 ($\beta = -0.332$; $p < 0.000$) and 0.52 ($\beta = -0.656$; $p < 0.000$), respectively. Increased locus of control also decreases the odds of being in trouble with the police since Wave 1 by a factor of 0.65 ($\beta = -0.430$; $p < 0.000$).[3] In terms of percent change, for a standard deviation change in locus of control, involvement in violence and drug dealing are expected to decrease by 26.54% and 45.63%, respectively. Trouble with police is also expected to decrease by 32.93% for a standard deviation change in locus of control.[4]

Model 1b: Influence of Locus of Control on Crime by Neighborhoods

Model 1b examines whether the influence of locus of control on crime varies by neighborhood (Table 15). According to the intercept coefficients, expected involvement in violence decreases by 0.49 ($p < 0.000$) and expected involvement in drug dealing decreases by 3.21 ($p < 0.000$). Further, trouble with police is decreased by 1.88 ($p < 0.000$), holding locus of control constant.[5]

Compared to other youths in the neighborhood, youths with an average locus of control score are 0.72 ($\beta = -0.326$; $p < 0.000$) times less likely to engage in violent behaviors and 0.59 ($\beta = -0.526$; $p < 0.000$) times less likely to engage in drug dealing. Having an average level of locus of control also decreases a youth's likelihood of being in trouble with police by 0.66 ($\beta = -0.413$; $p < 0.000$).[6] In terms of percent change, for a standard deviation change in locus of control, involvement in violence and drug dealing are expected to decrease by 26.13% and 38.65%, respectively. Trouble with police is also expected to decrease by 31.86% for a standard deviation change in locus of control.

Table 14. Model 1a: Influence of locus of control on crime

PHDCN Data, N = 1,764

	Violence Scale			Drug Dealing Scale			Trouble with Police		
	b	SE	Event Rate Ratio	b	SE	Event Rate Ratio	b	SE	Odds Ratio
Intercept	-0.500***	0.060	0.606	-3.278***	0.162	0.038	-1.897***	0.080	0.150
Locus of Control	-0.332***	0.046	0.717	-0.656***	0.119	0.519	-0.430***	0.065	0.650

*** $p < 0.000$

Table 15. Model 1b: Influence of locus of control on crime by neighborhoods

PHDCN Data, N = 1,764

	Violence Scale			Drug Dealing Scale			Trouble with Police		
	b	SE	Event Rate Ratio	b	SE	Event Rate Ratio	b	SE	Odds Ratio
Intercept	-0.494***	0.062	0.610	-3.206***	0.120	0.040	-1.880***	0.076	0.153
Locus of Control	-0.326***	0.049	0.722	-0.526***	0.091	0.591	-0.413***	0.065	0.662

Variance Components

		St. Dev.	Variance	df	χ^2
Violence Scale	Intercept	0.363	0.132	75	132.370***
	Locus of Control	0.184	0.034	75	73.753
Drug Dealing Scale	Intercept	0.772	0.596	75	107.265**
	Locus of Control	0.542	0.294	75	80.929
Trouble with Police	Intercept	0.337	0.114	75	94.631
	Locus of Control	0.195	0.038	75	75.832

* $p < 0.05$ ** $p < 0.01$ *** $p < 0.000$

Comparing the findings from Models 1a and 1b, there appear to be no neighborhood differences with regard to the relationship between locus of control and violence, drug dealing, and trouble with the police. The chi-square tests indicate that there is good model fit for the trouble with police outcome, but that a one-factor model is an insufficient explanation of violence and drug dealing.

Model 1c: Influence of Locus of Control on Crime – Controlling for Individual-Level Variables

Model 1c builds on Model 1a[7] by controlling for the following individual-level characteristics: cohort, sex, and race/ethnicity (Table 16). After adding these control variables to the model, the intercepts remain statistically significant. Expected involvement in violence, drug dealing, and trouble with police are decreased by 1.69 ($p < 0.000$), 6.50 ($p < 0.000$), and 3.59 ($p < 0.000$), respectively, when all other coefficients are held constant.

Locus of control remains statistically significant in this model. Compared to other youths in the neighborhood, youths with an average level of locus of control are 0.73 ($\beta = -0.315$; $p < 0.000$) times less likely to engage in violent behaviors, 0.62 ($\beta = -0.472$; $p < 0.000$) times less likely to be involved in drug dealing, and 0.68 ($\beta = -0.386$; $p < 0.000$) times less likely to be in trouble with the police. For a standard deviation change in locus of control, violence is expected to decrease by 25.37%, drug dealing is expected to decrease by 35.49%, and trouble with police is expected to decrease by 30.13%.

Cohort membership (Cohort 12 and Cohort 15) was entered into the model.[8] Compared to youths in Cohort 9, being in Cohort 12 or Cohort 15 is positively and significantly related to involvement in violence, drug dealing, and trouble with the police. Compared to Cohort 9, being in Cohort 12 increases a youth's expected involvement in violence by 2.51 ($\beta = 0.921$; $p < 0.000$), drug dealing by 16.58 ($\beta = 2.808$; $p < 0.01$), and trouble with police by 3.01 ($\beta = 1.101$; $p < 0.000$). Compared to youths in Cohort 9, belonging to Cohort 12 is expected to increase involvement in violence, drug dealing, and trouble with police by 151.18%, 1557.67%, and 200.72%, respectively. Compared to Cohort 9, membership in Cohort 15 increases a youth's expected involvement in violence by 3.08 ($\beta = 1.124$; $p < 0.000$), drug dealing by 65.25 ($\beta = 4.178$; $p < 0.000$), and trouble with the police by 7.30 ($\beta = 1.988$; $p < 0.000$). In terms of percent change, compared to youths in Cohort 9, being in Cohort 15 is expected to increase involvement in violence, drug dealing, and trouble with police by 207.71%, 6423.52%,[9] and 630.09%, respectively. There is an obvious increase in expected involvement in the three self-reported offending behaviors among older youths in Cohorts 12 and 15 compared to younger youths in Cohort 9.

Models incorporating age and age-squared was also employed (complete data not shown). There were no substantive changes between the violence scale model including age and age-squared and the model excluding these variables. There were three substantive changes in the drug dealing scale between the two models. Once age and age-squared were removed, the intercept coefficient became significant and the coefficients for Cohort 12 and Cohort 15 changed direction and became significant (as shown in Table 16). The coefficients for these variables in the drug dealing scale model incorporating age and age-squared were: intercept ($\beta = -31.674$; $p > 0.05$), Cohort 12 ($\beta = -0.035$; $p > 0.05$), and Cohort 15 ($\beta = -0.021$; $p > 0.05$). The same changes occurred in the trouble with police model. The coefficients for these variables in the trouble with police model incorporating age and age-squared were: intercept ($\beta = -9.499$; $p > 0.05$), Cohort 12 ($\beta = -0.189$; $p > 0.05$), and Cohort 15 ($\beta = -0.509$; $p > 0.05$). Age and age-squared were dropped from the model because these variables are confounded with cohort membership.

Male is significantly related to involvement in violence, drug dealing, and trouble with police. Compared to females, being male increases a youth's expected involvement in violence by 1.71 ($\beta = 0.539$; $p < 0.000$), drug dealing by 2.11 ($\beta = 0.749$; $p < 0.01$), and trouble with police by 2.56 ($\beta = 0.942$; $p < 0.000$). Expected involvement in violence,

Table 16. Model 1c: Influence of locus of control on crime – Controlling for individual-level variables

PHDCN Data, N = 1,726

	Violence Scale			Drug Dealing Scale			Trouble with Police		
	b	SE	Event Rate Ratio	b	SE	Event Rate Ratio	b	SE	Odds Ratio
Intercept	-1.691***	0.155	0.184	-6.499***	0.923	0.002	-3.586***	0.252	0.028
Locus of Control	-0.315***	0.050	0.729	-0.472***	0.121	0.624	-0.386***	0.067	0.680
Cohort 12	0.921***	0.127	2.513	2.808**	0.911	16.571	1.101***	0.231	3.006
Cohort 15	1.124***	0.128	3.077	4.178***	0.849	65.248	1.988***	0.209	7.298
Male	0.539***	0.102	1.715	0.749**	0.242	2.116	0.942***	0.137	2.565
African American	0.529***	0.142	1.698	-0.136	0.305	0.873	0.353	0.186	1.423
Hispanic	-0.218	0.134	0.804	-1.083	0.285	0.339	-0.394	0.204	0.674

Variance Components

		St. Dev.	Variance	df	χ^2
Violence Scale	Intercept	0.177	0.031	78	99.594*
Drug Dealing Scale	Intercept	0.763	0.583	78	146.305***
Trouble with Police	Intercept	0.168	0.028	78	83.335

$* p < 0.05 ** p < 0.01 *** p < 0.000$

drug dealing, and trouble with police increases by 71.43%, 111.49%, and 156.51%, respectively, for males compared to females.

African American is also significantly related to expected involvement in violence. Compared to youths of other races/ethnicities, African Americans are 1.70 ($\beta = 0.529$; $p <$ 0.000) times more likely to be involved in violence than youths of other races/ethnicities. Expected involvement in violence is increased by 69.72% for African Americans. In this model, African American is not related to drug dealing or trouble with police. Compared to other races/ethnicities, Hispanic is not related to any of the outcomes.

Model 1d: Influence of Locus of Control on Crime – Controlling for Individual-Level Variables, Neighborhood Context, and Family Context

Model 1d adds neighborhood context and family context variables to Model 1c. The intercepts in Model 1d remain statistically significant (Table 17). Expected involvement in violence is decreased by 1.26 ($p < 0.05$), drug dealing is decreased by 4.77 ($p < 0.000$), and trouble with the police is decreased by 3.02 ($p < 0.000$) when all other coefficients are held constant.

In this model the influence of neighborhood context variables on the intercept is investigated. One question of interest is whether involvement in crime varies by neighborhood context.[10] The results indicate that neighborhood SES is significantly related to a decrease in violence and drug dealing. Compared to youths in other neighborhoods, youths living in average SES neighborhoods are 0.88 ($\beta = -0.129$; $p < 0.05$) times less likely to report involvement in violent behaviors and 0.65 ($\beta = -0.433$; $p < 0.01$) times less likely to engage in drug dealing. In terms of percent change, for a standard deviation change in neighborhood SES, involvement in violence and drug dealing are expected to decrease by 16.78% and 29.28%, respectively. Neighborhood SES does not influence trouble with police, and neighborhood level ethnic heterogeneity, residential mobility, and family disruption do not influence individual involvement in any of the behaviors.

Locus of control remains statistically significant and negatively related to violence, drug dealing, and trouble with the police. Youths with an average level of locus of control are 0.71 (β = -0.344; p < 0.000), 0.64 (β = -0.453; p < 0.01), and 0.67 (β = -0.397; p < 0.000) times less likely to engage in violence or drug dealing or be in trouble with police, respectively. For a standard deviation change in locus of control, involvement in violence is expected to decrease by 27.35% and drug dealing is expected to decrease by 34.25%. Trouble with police is expected to decrease by 30.84% for each standard deviation change in locus of control.

Third, in this model the influence of family context variables on youths' involvement in violence, drug dealing, and trouble with the police is investigated. Relative to youths whose primary caregiver was born in the United States, having a primary caregiver who is a first generation immigrant significantly decreases a youth's expected involvement in violence by 0.72 (β = -0.330; p < 0.05), but does not influence drug dealing or trouble with the police. Youths who have a primary caregiver who is a first generation immigrant are expected to have 28.11% less involvement in violence than youths whose parents were born in the United States.

Having a primary caregiver who is separated or divorced decreases a youth's expected involvement in violence by 0.77 (β = -0.266; p < 0.05), compared to youths not experiencing family disruption. In terms of percent change, experiencing family disruption is expected to decrease involvement in violence by 23.36%. Family disruption does not influence drug dealing or trouble with police.

A larger family size is positively and significantly related to trouble with police, but is unrelated to violence and drug dealing. Compared to youths in smaller families, residing with a larger family increases a youths expected trouble with the police by

1.11 ($\beta = 0.107$; $p < 0.01$). For a standard deviation change in family size, the likelihood of a youth being in trouble with the police increases by 23.99%. Family SES and parental monitoring do not influence any of the outcomes.

Finally, individual-level variables are also included in this model. Belonging to Cohort 12 or Cohort 15 is positively and significantly related to involvement in violence, drug dealing, and trouble with police. Compared to youths in Cohort 9, youths in Cohort 12 are 2.55 ($\beta = 0.937$; $p < 0.000$) and youths in Cohort 15 are 3.13 ($\beta = 1.140$; $p < 0.000$) times more likely to engage in violence. Compared to youths in Cohort 9, youths in Cohort 12 are 11.87 ($\beta = 2.474$; $p < 0.01$) and youths in Cohort 15 are 55.30 ($\beta = 4.013$; $p < 0.000$) times more likely to report involvement in drug dealing. Youths in Cohort 12 are 3.09 ($\beta = 1.129$; $p < 0.000$) and youths in Cohort 15 are 7.35 ($\beta = 1.994$; $p < 0.000$) times more likely to be in trouble with the police compared to youths in Cohort 9. In terms of percent change, compared to youths in Cohort 9, membership in Cohort 12 is expected to increase involvement in violence by 155.23%, drug dealing by 1086.98%, and trouble with the police by 209.26%. Similarly, belonging to Cohort 15 is expected to increase involvement in violence by 212.68%, drug dealing by 5431.25%, and trouble with the police by 634.48%.

Models incorporating age and age-squared was also employed (complete data not shown). There were two substantive changes in the violence scale between the two models. Once age and age-squared were removed, the intercept and family disruption coefficients became significant. The coefficients for these variables in the violence scale model incorporating age and age-squared were: intercept ($\beta = -6.308$; $p > 0.05$) and family disruption ($\beta = -0.259$; $p > 0.05$). There were eight changes in the drug dealing scale between the two models. Once age and age-squared were removed, four coefficients became significant. These are for the intercept, Cohort 12, Cohort 15, and Hispanic. The coefficients for these variables in the drug dealing scale model incorporating age and age-squared were: intercept (β = -29.043; p > 0.05), Cohort 12 (β = -0.378; p > 0.05), Cohort 15 (β = -1.064; p > 0.05), and Hispanic (β = -0.408; p > 0.05). The coefficients for Cohort 12 and Cohort 15 also changed from negative to positive with the removal of age and age-squared. Four additional coefficients changed from positive to negative (neighborhood residential mobility, neighborhood family disruption, family disruption, and family size), but remained non-significant. For the trouble with police model, there were three substantive changes between the two models. Once age and age-squared were removed, the intercept, Cohort 12, and Cohort 15 coefficients became significant. The coefficients for these variables in the trouble with police model incorporating age and age-squared were: intercept (β = -8.696; p > 0.05), Cohort 12 (β = -0.378; p > 0.05), and Cohort 15 (β = -1.064; p > 0.05). The coefficients for Cohort 12 and Cohort 15 also changed from negative to positive. As with Model 1c, age and age-squared were not included in the final model because they are confounded with cohort membership.

Males are more likely to be involved in violence, drug dealing, and trouble with the police than females. It is expected that males' involvement in violence and drug dealing, and trouble with police will be 1.74 (β = 0.553; p < 0.000), 2.61 (β = 0.958; p < 0.000), and 2.62 (β = 0.965; p < 0.000) times greater than that of females, respectively. Expected involvement in violence, drug dealing, and trouble with police increased by 73.85%, 160.65%, and 162.48%, respectively, for males compared to females.

Race/ethnicity is also examined. Compared to other races/ethnicities, youths who are African American are 1.50 (β = 0.408; p < 0.01) times more likely to engage in violence than youths of other races/ethnicities, and expected involvement in violence increases by 50.38% for African Americans. On the other hand, Hispanic youths are 0.32 (β = -1.123; p < 0.01) times less likely to be involved in drug dealing than other youths. Expected involvement in drug dealing decreased by 67.47% among Hispanic youths. Race/ethnicity was not related to trouble with police.

Table 17. Model 1d: Influence of locus of control on crime – Controlling for individual-level variables, neighborhood context, and family context

PHDCN Data, N = 1,767

	Violence Scale			Drug Dealing Scale			Trouble with Police		
	b	SE	Event Rate Ratio	b	SE	Event Rate Ratio	b	SE	Odds Ratio
Intercept	-1.256*	0.510	0.285	-4.774 ***	1.242	0.008	-3.016***	0.781	0.049
Neighborhood Residential Mobility	0.143	0.126	1.154	-0.273	0.238	0.761	0.211	0.187	1.235
Neighborhood SES	-0.129*	0.064	0.879	-0.433**	0.154	0.649	-0.130	0.115	0.878
Neighborhood Ethnic Heterogeneity	-0.005	0.032	0.995	0.118	0.065	1.125	0.001	0.043	1.001
Neighborhood Family Disruption	-0.136	0.704	0.873	-1.309	1.262	0.270	0.721	1.060	2.057
Locus of Control	-0.344***	0.054	0.709	-0.453**	0.132	0.638	-0.397***	0.076	0.674
PC Immigrant Status	-0.330*	0.155	0.719	-0.209	0.388	0.811	-0.421	0.229	0.656
Family SES	-0.020	0.042	0.980	-0.160	0.109	0.852	-0.043	0.068	0.957
Family Disruption	-0.266*	0.134	0.766	-0.164	0.262	0.848	0.051	0.198	1.052
Family Size	0.015	0.026	1.016	-0.101	0.089	0.904	0.107**	0.040	1.113
Parental Monitoring	-0.016	0.018	0.984	-0.043	0.036	0.958	-0.050	0.034	0.953

Table 17, continued. Model 1d: Influence of locus of control on crime – Controlling for individual-level variables, neighborhood context, and family context

PHDCN Data, N = 1,767

	Violence Scale			Drug Dealing Scale			Trouble with Police		
	b	SE	Event Rate Ratio	b	SE	Event Rate Ratio	b	SE	Odds Ratio
Cohort 12	0.937***	0.138	2.554	2.474**	0.897	11.876	1.129***	0.246	3.094
Cohort 15	1.140***	0.142	3.128	4.013***	0.819	55.297	1.994***	0.236	7.349
Male	0.553***	0.108	1.739	0.958***	0.241	2.601	0.965***	0.151	2.625
African American	0.408**	0.158	1.504	-0.037	0.357	0.964	0.025	0.214	1.026
Hispanic	-0.122	0.181	0.885	-1.123**	0.376	0.325	-0.382	0.314	0.683

Variance Components

		St. Dev.	Variance	df	χ^2
Violence Scale	Intercept	0.223	0.049	74	88.517
Drug Dealing Scale	Intercept	0.879	0.772	74	163.777***
Trouble with Police	Intercept	0.243	0.059	74	79.937

* $p < 0.05$ ** $p < 0.01$ *** $p < 0.000$

RESEARCH QUESTION 2: DOES COLLECTIVE EFFICACY INFLUENCE SELF-REPORTED INVOLVEMENT IN CRIME?

Model 2a: Influence of Collective Efficacy on Crime

According to the intercept coefficients, when collective efficacy is held constant expected involvement in drug dealing decreases by 3.76 ($p < 0.05$) and being in trouble with police decreases by 2.84 ($p < 0.01$). The intercept for violence is not significant. Contrary to the hypothesis, neighborhood collective efficacy does not influence individual-level involvement in violence, drug dealing, or trouble with the police (Table 18). Reported results are from the population-average model with robust standard errors. The event rate ratios for the violence and drug dealing scales and the odds ratio for trouble with police are not significant.

Model 2b: Influence of Collective Efficacy on Crime Involvement – Controlling for Neighborhood Context and Family

Model 2b examines the influence of collective efficacy on crime involvement while controlling for neighborhood context and family context. Individual-level demographic variables (cohort, sex, and race/ethnicity) are not expected to influence the relationship between collective efficacy and crime involvement, and therefore are not included in this model. In this model, none of the intercepts are significant (Table 19). Contrary to the hypotheses tested in this study and the extant literature, none of the neighborhood context variables are related to the violence scale, drug dealing scale, or trouble with the police.

Turning to the family context variables, youths whose primary caregiver is a first generation immigrant are less likely to engage in violence and be in trouble with the police.

Table 18. Model 2a: Influence of collective efficacy on crime

PHDCN Data, N = 1,764

	Violence Scale			Drug Dealing Scale			Trouble with Police		
	b	SE	Event Rate Ratio	b	SE	Event Rate Ratio	b	SE	Odds Ratio
Intercept	-0.478	0.615	0.620	-3.756*	1.519	0.023	-2.843**	0.819	0.058
Collective Efficacy	0.008	0.178	1.008	0.203	0.435	1.225	0.292	0.233	1.339

* $p < 0.05$ ** $p < 0.01$ *** $p < 0.000$

Table 19. Model 2b: Influence of collective efficacy on crime – Controlling for neighborhood context and family context

PHDCN Data, N = 1,767

	Violence Scale			Drug Dealing Scale			Trouble with Police		
	b	SE	Event Rate Ratio	b	SE	Event Rate Ratio	b	SE	Odds Ratio
Intercept	-0.885	1.122	0.413	-1.374	3.145	0.253	-3.076	1.717	0.046
Neighborhood Residential Mobility	0.123	0.173	1.131	-0.268	0.352	0.765	0.399	0.207	1.492
Neighborhood SES	-0.131	0.089	0.877	-0.114	0.214	0.892	-0.011	0.162	0.988
Neighborhood Ethnic Heterogeneity	-0.029	0.041	0.971	0.079	0.077	1.082	-0.059	0.051	0.943
Neighborhood Family Disruption	-0.070	0.776	0.932	-0.759	1.907	0.468	0.811	0.955	2.251
Neighborhood Collective Efficacy	0.111	0.286	1.117	-0.184	0.805	0.832	0.173	0.488	1.189
Immigrant Status	-0.554**	0.154	0.575	-0.562	0.404	0.569	-0.514*	0.210	0.598
Family SES	0.001	0.067	1.001	0.030	0.161	1.031	0.104	0.077	1.109
Family Disruption	0.018	0.201	1.019	0.199	0.379	1.220	0.589**	0.206	1.804
Family Size	0.033	0.042	1.034	-0.124	0.172	0.884	0.118*	0.048	1.125
Parental Monitoring	-0.085**	0.025	0.919	-0.163***	0.041	0.849	-0.136**	0.041	0.872

Table 19, continued. Model 2b: Influence of collective efficacy on crime – Controlling for neighborhood context and family context

PHDCN Data, N = 1,767

Variance Components

		St. Dev.	Variance	df	χ^2
Violence Scale	Intercept	0.163	0.026	71	66.973
Drug Dealing Scale	Intercept	0.133	0.018	71	60.109
Trouble with Police	Intercept	0.088	0.008	71	79.414

* $p < 0.05$ ** $p < 0.01$ *** $p < 0.000$

Compared to youths whose primary caregiver was born in the United States, having a primary caregiver who is a first generation immigrant significantly reduces expected involvement in violence by 0.57 ($\beta = -0.554$; $p < 0.01$) and also decreases the odds of being in trouble with police by 0.60 ($\beta = -0.514$; $p < 0.05$). In terms of percent change, involvement in violence and trouble with police are expected to decrease by 42.53% and 40.19%, respectively.

Family disruption is positively and significantly related to being in trouble with the police. Youths whose primary caregiver is separated or divorced have 1.80 ($\beta = 0.589$; $p < 0.01$) greater odds of being in trouble with the police than youths whose primary caregiver is single, married, widowed, or lives with their partner. Youths experiencing family disruption have an 80.22% increased likelihood of being in trouble with the police than other young persons.

Family size is positively and significantly related to being in trouble with the police. An increase in family size increases a youth's odds of being in trouble with police by 1.12 ($\beta = 0.118$; $p < 0.05$), compared to youths who reside with a smaller family. For each standard deviation increase in family size, trouble with police is expected to increase by 26.77%.

There is a negative and significant relationship between parental monitoring and all three outcomes. Youths experiencing average levels of parental monitoring are 0.92 ($\beta = -0.085$; $p < 0.01$) times less likely to report involvement in violent behaviors, 0.85 ($\beta = -0.163$; $p < 0.000$) times less likely to engage in drug dealing, and 0.87 ($\beta = -0.136$; $p < 0.01$) times less likely to be in trouble with the police. For a standard deviation change in parental monitoring, expected involvement in violence decreases by 19.35% and expected drug dealing decreases by 33.79%. Expected trouble with police decreases by 29.11% for each standard deviation change in parental monitoring.

RESEARCH QUESTION 3: DOES COLLECTIVE EFFICACY
MODERATE THE RELATIONSHIP BETWEEN LOCUS OF
CONTROL AND SELF-REPORTED INVOLVEMENT IN CRIME?

The next section of this chapter explores the relationship
between locus of control and collective efficacy. The first model
(3a) examines the influence of collective efficacy and locus of
control on crime involvement. The second model (3b) examines
whether collective efficacy moderates the relationship between
crime involvement and locus of control. The final model (3c)
includes contextual variables (neighborhood context and family
context) and individual-level variables (cohort, sex, and
race/ethnicity) believed to influence crime involvement.

**Model 3a: Relationship between Collective Efficacy, Locus of
Control, and Crime**

Model 3a examines the relationship of both collective efficacy
and locus of control on involvement in crime (Table 20).
According to the intercepts, drug dealing decreases by 4.09
($p < 0.01$) and trouble with police decreases by 2.78 ($p < 0.01$)
when all other variables are held constant. The intercept for
violence is not significant.

Collective efficacy does not influence involvement in any of
the three outcomes. Locus of control remains negatively related
to involvement in violence, drug dealing, and trouble with
police. Expected involvement in violence and drug dealing in the
12 months before the interview among youths with an average
level of locus of control is decreased by 0.72 ($\beta = -0.328$;
$p < 0.000$) and 0.52 ($\beta = -0.648$; $p < 0.000$), respectively.
Expected trouble with police since the Wave 1 interview among
youths with an average level of locus of control decreases by
0.66 ($\beta = -0.418$; $p < 0.000$). In terms of percent change, for a
standard deviation change in locus of control, involvement in
violence, drug dealing, and trouble with police are expected to
decrease by 26.27%, 45.23%, and 32.18%, respectively.

Table 20. Model 3a: Relationship between collective efficacy, locus of control, and crime

PHDCN Data, N = 1,767

Variable	Violence Scale			Drug Dealing Scale			Trouble with Police		
	b	SE	Event Rate Ratio	b	SE	Event Rate Ratio	b	SE	Odds Ratio
Average Crime									
Intercept	-0.435	0.627	0.647	-4.088**	1.243	0.017	-2.778**	0.847	0.062
Collective Efficacy	-0.019	0.181	0.981	0.238	0.365	1.269	0.258	0.239	1.295
Locus of Control Slope									
Intercept	-0.328***	0.051	0.720	-0.648***	0.125	0.523	-0.418***	0.069	0.658

Variance Components

	St. Dev.	Variance	df	χ^2
Violence Scale	Intercept	0.328	0.107	77	126.264**
Drug Dealing Scale	Intercept	0.454	0.206	77	72.946
Trouble with Police	Intercept	0.225	0.051	77	95.029

* $p < 0.05$ ** $p < 0.01$ *** $p < 0.000$

Model 3b: Moderating Effect of Collective Efficacy on the Relationship between Locus of Control, and Crime

Model 3b examines whether collective efficacy moderates the relationship between locus of control and crime which was found to be significant for the three outcomes in Models 1a, 1b, 1c, and 1d. First, as was found in Model 3a, two intercepts were significant; drug dealing decreases by 4.92 ($p < 0.01$) and trouble with police decreases by 2.69 ($p < 0.01$), when all other variables are held constant (Table 21). The intercept for violence is not significant.

Second, by testing a moderation effect, I seek to determine whether the relationship between locus of control and crime changes as a function of collective efficacy. Moderation occurs if the relationship between the independent variable and outcome variable increases or decreases with the addition of the moderating variable. Moderation can also occur when a relationship between the independent variable and outcome variable is no longer apparent once the moderating variable is introduced (Baron and Kenny, 1986). Multilevel models are useful for determining whether an individual factor (locus of control) is moderated by a macro-level variable such as collective efficacy (see Taylor, 2010).

It is hypothesized that the influence of locus of control on crime will increase and become stronger by interacting locus of control and collective efficacy. A test of the moderator effects of collective efficacy is supported by the findings reported thus far. According to Baron and Kenny (1986), moderator variables should be uncorrelated to the independent and outcome variables; collective efficacy meets this key criterion. The correlation between collective efficacy and locus of control is 0.082, and the correlations between collective efficacy and violence, drug dealing, and trouble with police are 0.001, 0.011, and 0.028, respectively.

Table 21. Model 3b: Moderating effect of collective efficacy on the relationship between locus of control and crime

PHDCN Data, N = 1,767

Variable	Violence Scale			Drug Dealing Scale			Trouble with Police		
	b	SE	Event Rate Ratio	b	SE	Event Rate Ratio	b	SE	Odds Ratio
Average Crime									
Intercept	-0.324	0.647	0.723	-4.923**	1.348	0.007	-2.686**	0.915	0.068
Collective Efficacy	-0.052	0.187	0.949	0.480	0.392	1.616	0.232	0.260	1.262
Locus of Control slope									
Intercept	0.039	0.471	1.039	-1.837	1.020	0.159	-0.065	0.716	0.937
Locus of Control x Collective Efficacy	-0.107	0.140	0.898	0.348	0.300	1.417	-0.102	0.206	0.903

Table 21, continued. Model 3b: Moderating effect of collective efficacy on the relationship between locus of control and crime

PHDCN Data, N = 1,767

Variance Components

		St. Dev.	Variance	df	χ^2
Violence Scale	Intercept	0.327	0.107	77	126.091**
Drug Dealing Scale	Intercept	0.415	0.172	77	70.384
Trouble with Police	Intercept	0.223	0.049	77	94.763

* $p < 0.05$ ** $p < 0.01$ *** $p < 0.000$

An interaction term is added by modeling collective efficacy on the locus of control coefficient to determine if the relationship between locus of control and crime is dependent on collective efficacy. Collective efficacy completely moderates the relationships between locus of control and crime involvement (Table 21).[11] The previously significant relationships between locus of control and the crime outcomes disappear when locus of control is interacted with collective efficacy, resulting in complete moderation. Here, complete moderation occurs because the causal effect of locus of control on crime involvement disappears when collective efficacy is added to the model. Contrary to the hypotheses, the interaction between locus of control and collective efficacy does not influence youths' involvement in crime. The influence of locus of control on involvement in crime is not different for youths living in neighborhoods with higher levels of collective efficacy than it is for youths living in neighborhoods with lower levels of collective efficacy. In simpler terms, the relationship between locus of control and crime involvement does not depend on collective efficacy.

Model 3c: Moderating Effect of Collective Efficacy on the Relationship between Locus of Control, and Crime – Controlling for Individual-Level Variables, Neighborhood Context, and Family Context

Model 3c builds on Model 3b by examining the influence of neighborhood context, family context, and individual-level factors on the moderating model.

Similar to Models 3a and 3b, two intercepts were significant. According to the intercepts, drug dealing decreases by 5.35 ($p < 0.05$) and trouble with police decreases by 6.11 ($p < 0.000$), when all other variables are held constant (Table 22). The intercept for violence is not significant.

In this model, locus of control does not influence youths' involvement in crime. As in Model 3b, collective efficacy moderates the relationship between locus of control and crime (Table 22).

Table 22. Model 3c: Moderating effect of collective efficacy on the relationship between locus of control and crime – Controlling for individual-level variables, neighborhood context, and family context

PHDCN Data, N = 1,767

	Violence Scale			Drug Dealing Scale			Trouble with Police		
	b	SE	Event Rate Ratio	b	SE	Event Rate Ratio	b	SE	Odds Ratio
Intercept	-2.124	1.075	0.119	-5.354*	2.570	0.005	-6.107***	1.606	0.002
Neighborhood Residential Mobility	0.194	0.136	1.214	-0.257	0.245	0.773	0.398*	0.191	1.489
Neighborhood SES	-0.178*	0.071	0.837	-0.412*	0.179	0.662	-0.298*	0.131	0.743
Neighborhood Ethnic Heterogeneity	-0.004	0.032	0.995	0.113	0.066	1.119	0.006	0.044	1.006
Neighborhood Family Disruption	-0.059	0.726	0.942	-1.235	1.375	0.291	1.035	1.113	2.815
Neighborhood Collective Efficacy	0.244	0.229	1.276	0.169	0.626	1.185	0.870*	0.390	2.388
Locus of Control	-0.464	0.511	0.628	-1.862	1.127	0.155	-0.634	0.748	0.530
Locus of Control x Collective Efficacy	0.035	0.152	1.036	0.415	0.336	1.515	0.069	0.218	1.071
Immigrant Status	-0.314*	0.153	0.730	-0.251	0.393	0.778	-0.358	0.225	0.699

Table 22, continued. Model 3c: Moderating effect of collective efficacy on the relationship between locus of control and crime – Controlling for individual-level variables, neighborhood context, and family context

PHDCN Data, N = 1,767

	Violence Scale			Drug Dealing Scale			Trouble with Police		
	b	SE	Event Rate Ratio	b	SE	Event Rate Ratio	b	SE	Odds Ratio
Family SES	-0.018	0.042	0.982	-0.157	0.107	0.855	-0.035	0.067	0.967
Family Disruption	-0.264	0.135	0.768	-0.170	0.266	0.843	0.064	0.198	1.066
Family Size	0.016	0.027	1.016	-0.101	0.088	0.904	0.110**	0.040	1.116
Parental Monitoring	-0.016	0.018	0.984	-0.044	0.035	0.956	-0.052	0.033	0.949
Cohort 12	0.937***	0.137	2.552	2.481**	0.885	11.953	1.119***	0.247	3.062
Cohort 15	1.139***	0.140	3.124	4.014***	0.806	55.399	1.988***	0.238	7.299
Male	0.552***	0.108	1.738	0.996***	0.237	2.708	0.962***	0.151	2.617
African American	0.428**	0.159	1.534	-0.023	0.345	0.978	0.119	0.214	1.127
Hispanic	-0.112	0.181	0.894	-1.134**	0.383	0.322	-0.337	0.317	0.713

Table 22, continued. Model 3c: Moderating effect of collective efficacy on the relationship between locus of control and crime – Controlling for individual-level variables, neighborhood context, and family context

PHDCN Data, N = 1,767

Variance Components

		St. Dev.	Variance	df	χ^2
Violence Scale	Intercept	0.226	0.051	73	87.829
Drug Dealing Scale	Intercept	0.898	0.807	73	166.684***
Trouble with Police	Intercept	0.183	0.033	73	76.871

* $p < 0.05$ ** $p < 0.01$ *** $p < 0.000$

The relationship between the interaction term (collective efficacy x locus of control) is positively related to all three outcomes, though these relationships are not statistically significant. The relationship between locus of control and violence, drug dealing, and trouble with the police is substantially reduced when locus of control is interacted with collective efficacy. Models 1a, 1b, 1c, and 1d show a significant and negative relationship between locus of control and the crime involvement outcomes, and these relationships disappear in Models 3b and 3c when collective efficacy is introduced as a moderating variable.

Neighborhood residential mobility is positively and significantly related to being in trouble with the police. Youths living in neighborhoods with an average level of residential mobility are 1.49 ($\beta = 0.398$; $p < 0.05$) times more likely to be in trouble with the police since the Wave 1 interview than youths living in neighborhoods with below or above average mobility. For a standard deviation change in neighborhood residential mobility, the likelihood of being trouble with the police is expected to increase by 23.48%.

There is a statistically significant and negative relationship between neighborhood SES and involvement in violence, drug dealing, and trouble with police. Youths living in neighborhoods with an average SES are 0.84 ($\beta = -0.178$; $p < 0.05$), 0.66 ($\beta = -0.412$; $p < 0.05$), and 0.74 ($\beta = -0.298$; $p < 0.05$) times less likely to experience violence, drug dealing, and trouble with the police, respectively, than youths living in neighborhoods with either below or above average SES levels. In terms of percent change, for a standard deviation change in neighborhood SES, involvement in violence, drug dealing, and trouble with the police are expected to decrease by 13.27%, 28.08%, and 21.21%, respectively.

The final neighborhood context variable to be significantly related to crime involvement is collective efficacy. Neighborhood collective efficacy is positively related to trouble with the police. A unit increase in collective efficacy increases the odds of being in trouble with the police by 2.39 ($\beta = 0.870$; $p < 0.05$). In terms of percent change, for a standard deviation change in collective efficacy, trouble with the police is expected to increase by 28.70%. This is in contrast to the hypothesis that increased levels of collective efficacy will be related to a reduction in crime. Neighborhood ethnic heterogeneity and neighborhood family disruption are not related to any of the outcomes.

In this model, only two family context variables are significant. There is a significant and negative relationship between primary caregiver's immigrant status and involvement in violence. Youths with a primary caregiver who is a first generation immigrant are 0.73 ($\beta = -0.314$; $p < 0.05$) times less likely to engage in violence, compared to youths whose primary caregiver was born in the United States. Having a primary caregiver who is a first generation immigrant is expected to decrease involvement in violence by 26.95%.

There is also a positive and significant relationship between family size and trouble with the police. Compared to youths from smaller families, youths from a larger family are 1.12 ($\beta = 0.110$; $p < 0.01$) times more likely to be in trouble with the police. For a standard deviation change in family size, the odds of a youth being in trouble with the police increases by 24.74%.

Five individual-level variables are related to some involvement in crime. With respect to involvement in violence, youths in Cohort 12 are 2.55 ($\beta = 0.937$; $p < 0.000$) and youths in Cohort 15 are 3.12 ($\beta = 1.139$; $p < 0.000$) times more likely to engage in violent behaviors compared to youths in Cohort 9. Youths in Cohort 12 are 11.95 ($\beta = 2.481$; $p < 0.01$) and youths in Cohort 15 are 55.40 ($\beta = 4.014$; $p < 0.000$) times more likely to be involved in drug dealing compared to youths in Cohort 9. Similarly, youths in Cohort 12 are 3.06 ($\beta = 1.119$; $p < 0.000$) and youths in Cohort 15 are 7.30 ($\beta = 1.988$; $p < 0.000$) times more likely to be in trouble with the police compared to youths in Cohort 9. In terms of percent change, compared to youths in Cohort 9, belonging to Cohort 12 is expected to increase involvement in violence, drug dealing, and trouble with the police by 155.23%, 1095.32%, and 206.18%, respectively. Similarly, compared to youths in Cohort 9, membership in Cohort 15 is expected to increase involvement in violence, drug dealing, and trouble with the police by 212.36%, 5436.79%, and 630.09%, respectively.

Models incorporating age and age-squared were also employed (complete data not shown). There was one substantive change in the violence scale between the two models. Once age and age-squared were removed, the immigrant status coefficient became significant. The coefficient for this variable in the violence scale model incorporating age and age-squared was: immigrant status ($\beta = -0.303$; $p > 0.05$). There were six changes in the drug dealing scale between the two models. Once age and age-squared were removed, four coefficients became significant. These are for intercept, neighborhood SES, Cohort 12, and Cohort 15. The coefficients for these variables in the drug dealing scale model incorporating age and age-squared were: intercept ($\beta = -29.047$; $p > 0.05$), neighborhood SES ($\beta = -0.315$; $p > 0.05$), Cohort 12 ($\beta = -0.457$; $p > 0.05$), and Cohort 15 ($\beta = -0.555$; $p > 0.05$). Cohort 12 also changed from negative to positive with the removal of age and age-squared. The neighborhood ethnic heterogeneity coefficient became non-significant after age and age-squared were removed from the model. In the model incorporating age and age-squared, the coefficient was: ethnic heterogeneity ($\beta = 0.126$; $p < 0.05$). The family size coefficient changed to negative (but remained non-significant) from a positive coefficient in the age and age-squared model. For the trouble with police model, there were three substantive changes between the two models. Once age and age-squared were removed, the intercept, Cohort 12, and Cohort 15 coefficients became significant. The coefficients for these variables in the trouble with police model incorporating age and age-squared were: intercept ($\beta = -11.627$; $p > 0.05$), Cohort 12 ($\beta = -0.375$; $p > 0.05$), and Cohort 15 ($\beta = -1.041$; $p > 0.05$). The coefficients for Cohort 12 and Cohort 15 also changed from negative to positive.

Expected involvement in violence, drug dealing, and trouble with police is greater for males than females. Males are 1.74 ($\beta = 0.552$; $p < 0.000$), 2.71 ($\beta = 0.996$; $p < 0.000$), and 2.62 ($\beta = 0.962$; $p < 0.000$) times more likely to be involved in violence, drug dealing, or to be in trouble with the police, respectively, than females. Expected involvement in violence, drug dealing, and trouble with police increased by 73.67%, 170.74%, and 161.69%, respectively, for males compared to females.

Compared to youths of other races/ethnicities, African American youths are 1.53 ($\beta = 0.428$; $p < 0.01$) times more likely to be involved in violence (a 53.42% increase), while Hispanics are 0.32 ($\beta = -1.134$; $p < 0.01$) times less likely to be involved in drug dealing (a 67.83% decrease). Race/ethnicity is not related to trouble with the police.

CHAPTER FIVE
Conclusions and Implications

Most explanations of youth involvement in crime are at the micro- or macro-level, with few scholars attempting to incorporate both micro- and macro-level variables into a single explanation. For example, scholars have examined the independent influences of locus of control and collective efficacy on crime. Less attention has been paid to the relationship between locus of control and collective efficacy and how these constructs may jointly influence crime. This study investigates both the independent and combined influences of locus of control and collective efficacy on three measures of involvement in crime: violence, drug dealing, and trouble with the police. Specifically, the research examines three questions: 1) Does locus of control influence self-reported involvement in crime? 2) Does collective efficacy influence self-reported involvement in crime? and 3) Does collective efficacy moderate the relationship between locus of control and crime? Using data from three cohorts of youths ranging from 9 to 19 years of age who participated in the Project on Human Development in Chicago Neighborhoods three main conclusions can be drawn from the analyses.

First, an internal locus of control is negatively related to involvement in violence, drug dealing, and trouble with police, independent of neighborhood. Thus, as locus of control becomes more internal, expected involvement in violence, drug dealing, and trouble with the police significantly declines. These findings are congruent with other studies that examine the relationship between locus of control and crime involvement (e.g., Duke and Fenhagen, 1975; Lau and Leung, 1992; Marsa, O'Reilly, Carr, Murphy, O'Sullivan, Cotter, and Hevey, 2004; Obitz, Oziel, and Unmacht, 1973; Parrott and Strongman, 1984; Peiser and Heaven, 1996; Rotter, 1966) and extends explanation to more serious crimes rather than minor delinquent behaviors. Further, the findings emerge after controlling for neighborhood context (residential mobility, SES, ethnic heterogeneity, and family disruption), family context (primary caregiver's immigrant status, SES, family disruption, family size, and parental monitoring), and individual-level control variables (cohort, sex, and race/ethnicity). In other words, an internal locus of control orientation remains negatively related to the outcome variables after neighborhood context, family context, and individual-level variables are added to the models indicating the robustness of the findings.

These findings about the relationship between locus of control and youth involvement in crime add to the extant literature in several ways. This study addresses what Nagin (2007; see also Paternoster, Pogarsky, and Zimmerman, 2011) identified as a gap in the literature, individual choice and decision making regarding offending behavior, by examining locus of control as a mechanism that may explain the choice to engage in, or refrain from, crime. Locus of control was a popular social psychological explanation of crime and adaptation to incarceration in the late 1970s and early 1980s. However, its popularity has since waned and its potential to explain adolescents' choice to refrain from crime is untapped. This study revisits the relationship between locus of control and crime using a sample of youths living in Chicago neighborhoods and addresses some of the methodological issues surrounding early inquiries. For example, this study includes persons who have committed crime and those who have not; prior research often examined only offenders (e.g., Biggs et al., 1983; Bowen and Gilchrist, 2006; Cole and Kumchy, 1981; Cross and Tracy, 1971; Dekel et al., 2004; Hains and Herrman, 1989; Obitz et al., 1973;

Ollendick and Hersen, 1979). While other studies have taken advantage of small convenience samples (e.g., Duke and Fenhagen, 1975; Graham, 1993; Langdon and Talbot, 2006; Lederer et al., 1985; Marsa et al., 2004; Parrott and Strongman, 1984; Peiser and Heaven, 1996), this study examines a large sample of participants selected using stratified random probability sampling techniques. These techniques assure that all individuals in the neighborhoods had an equal chance of being selected for the study – thereby increasing generalizability of findings. This study also examines the neighborhood and family contexts that may influence involvement in crime, and takes advantage of the hierarchical nature of the data to test for neighborhood level differences of involvement in crime and locus of control. These methodological improvements add strength to the findings.

The second main finding is that collective efficacy for the most part does not influence individual-level involvement in violence, drug dealing, or trouble with the police contrary to expectation. However, one exception is documented in Model 3c. In this model, collective efficacy is positively and significantly related to trouble with the police since the Wave 1 interview. This relationship only emerges after all of the variables (neighborhood context, family context, individual-level variables, and interaction term between collective efficacy and locus of control) are added to the model.

While, in general, the hypothesis that neighborhood level collective efficacy influences individual-level involvement in crime is not supported by the current study, the findings are not surprising. Other studies using the PHDCN data also fail to uncover a significant relationship between collective efficacy and individual-level involvement in crime (Kirk, 2009; Molnar et al., 2008; Sampson et al., 2005; but see Maimon and Browning, 2010). Sampson et al. (2005) examined neighborhood predictors of self-reported violence and found similar results for similar neighborhood context variables. For example, collective efficacy, concentrated disadvantage[1] and residential stability were not significant predictors of violence among youth (see also Kirk, 2009). More consistent support exists for the influence of collective efficacy on crime rates (e.g., Browning, 2002; Sampson et al., 1997; Sampson and Raudenbush, 1999; see also Pratt and Cullen, 2005) than for the influence of collective efficacy on individual-level involvement in crime. Another potential explanation for the finding that collective efficacy does not influence youth involvement in crime is the fact that the collective efficacy measure (and other neighborhood-level variables) was collected between three and six years before Wave 2, when the locus of control and self-reported crime variables were captured (see section on Data Availability for a discussion on related implications).

The third main finding of this research is that collective efficacy completely moderates the relationships between locus of control and violence, drug dealing, and trouble with police,[2] though not in the expected direction. It was hypothesized that higher levels of collective efficacy would strengthen the influence of locus of control on violence, drug dealing, and trouble with police. However, according to the models, the level of collective efficacy in a youth's neighborhood does not strengthen these relationships. In fact, the relationships between locus of control and the outcomes are no longer significant when collective efficacy is added to the model. This unexpected finding is understandable since in this study collective efficacy does not influence individual-level crime and there is a weak correlation between locus of control and collective efficacy (0.082). Additional research is needed to investigate whether collective efficacy influences locus of control and if other neighborhood factors are related to locus of control.

A preliminary analysis of these relationships indicates that collective efficacy ($p < 0.01$) and neighborhood socioeconomic status ($p < 0.000$) are significantly and positively related to locus of control when each variable is examined as the only independent variable in the model. The other neighborhood factors (residential mobility, ethnic heterogeneity, and family disruption) are not related to locus of control. After adding all the neighborhood factors into one model, the relationship between locus of control and collective efficacy disappears. As noted earlier, the community measures may be misrepresenting what is currently occurring in the youths' neighborhoods since the data were collected at two different time points and neighborhoods can change over time (Bursik, 1986, 1988).

Baron and Kenny (1986: 1174) observe the following with regard to moderating variables: "At a conceptual level, a moderator may be more impressive if we go from a strong to a weak relation or to no relation at all as opposed to finding a crossover interaction." This is precisely what happened when collective efficacy was interacted with locus of control. The strong positive relationship between locus of control and crime involvement was nullified (no longer significant) with the addition of collective efficacy. The findings suggest that a multi-contextual approach does not appear to be necessary to explain the relationship between involvement in crime and locus of control. While not direct support, these findings may suggest that individual-level influences are more important than neighborhood factors for youth crime involvement. At the conceptual level, future research on the relationship between locus of control and youth involvement in crime can be informed by the results from this research. For example, scholars have postulated that "micro-communities" such as street segments or blocks may be more meaningful than neighborhoods when examining social disorganization and its relationship to social control over behavior (see Weisburd, 2012). Micro-communities may be more applicable than neighborhood contexts derived from census tracts, as examined in this research, for understanding contextual influences on the development of locus of control.

A secondary, yet interesting, finding from this study is the clustering of drug dealing in certain neighborhoods.[3] Unlike violence and trouble with police which are spread throughout more neighborhood clusters, drug dealing appears to be concentrated in a smaller number of neighborhood clusters. This concentration of drug dealing could be due to crime specialization in neighborhoods. For example, neighborhood clusters without any self-reported drug dealing may specialize in other types of crimes. At the macro-level, Schreck, McGloin, and Kirk (2009) found that PHDCN neighborhoods do experience crime specialization. Some neighborhoods appear to specialize in violence while non-violence is the norm in other neighborhoods. Additional research is needed to determine the causes of neighborhood specialization in crime-type and whether there is specialization at the micro-level.

LIMITATIONS AND AREAS OF FUTURE RESEARCH

The current study provides insight into the relationships between locus of control, collective efficacy, and crime. Overall, the study findings contribute to the literature by providing evidence that an internal locus of control negatively influences involvement in a variety of crimes. This research, however, is not without noteworthy limitations. Future research could build on this study, and address three such limitations in particular: data availability, measurement error, and omitted variable bias.

Data Availability

All studies based on secondary data, including the current one, are limited by the data available. For example, data available for analysis in this study somewhat dictates testing collective efficacy as having an enduring, rather than situational, effect on youth crime involvement. The argument for an enduring effect is based in socialization, while situational effects occur through monitoring. If collective efficacy has an enduring effect on behavior, the collective efficacy in the neighborhood where a youth lives will influence his or her behavior in other contexts, not only his or her neighborhood. If it is situational, the collective efficacy of a specific neighborhood (e.g., the one in which he or she lives) will only influence a youth's behavior if it occurs in that same neighborhood.

Because collective efficacy data were only collected during the Community Survey conducted in 1995 and locus of control is only available at Wave 2 (1997-2000) and Wave 3 (2000-2002), it is not possible to test a situational effect of collective efficacy on the outcomes in this study. Such a test would require additional data. First, contemporaneous measurements of collective efficacy and crime are necessary. In order to determine if collective efficacy influences a behavior at a given point in time, both variables should be captured in close proximity, but at distinct time points to retain the ability to predict causality. Further, it would be essential to know the neighborhood where a crime occurred and the level of collective efficacy in that neighborhood.

None of these variables are available in the current PHDCN data. This is a limitation to the current study because the extant literature shows evidence that the influence of collective efficacy is more situational than enduring at both the micro-level (Kirk, 2009; Sampson, 2006) and macro-level (Sampson et al., 1997). If collective efficacy indeed has a situational effect on behavior, this could explain why collective efficacy was not found to be related to involvement in crime and did not strengthen the relationship between locus of control and crime.

Longitudinal data is important to accurately measure neighborhood level factors such as social control and cohesion (Steenbeek and Hipp, 2011). Measuring collective efficacy at all three waves would have enabled this research to examine whether there had been changes in collective efficacy by neighborhood over time and if so, what impact those changes would have on the findings. Further, indicators of crime location would also enable scholars to test whether the impact of collective efficacy on crime is situational or enduring.

Measurement Error

A possible issue related to measurement error concerns the data available for this study. Due to the restricted data user's agreement with ICPSR, additional data sources (e.g., census data) could not be linked to the PHDCN data. This limitation resulted in some of the neighborhood context variables collected at the individual-level (i.e., residential mobility, socioeconomic status, and family disruption) being aggregated to the neighborhood cluster level to create a mean for each NC; this aggregation process results in the danger of involving the atomistic fallacy in the interpretation of results. This is because individual-level responses are used as indicators of neighborhood level variables; and the relationship between two variables at the individual-level may differ from the relationship between those variables had they been measured at the group level. While the results of the current research show that the majority of neighborhood context variables do not influence the outcomes, the inadequate measurement of these variables may contribute to the null findings.

Additionally, research suggests that levels of values and levels of informal social control may not be accurately assessed by community members and that these misperceptions may impact whether residents engage in informal social control. Warner and Burchfield (2011) found that people were less willing to intervene in situations they deemed inappropriate when they perceived their neighbors' values to be different from the values they held. The data set used in the current research contains variables that assess informal social control (as part of collective efficacy) but the surveys did not determine whether residents employed informal social controls based on the perceptions of their neighbors' values. Another important element is the influence of neighborhood context on perceptions of values. People are less likely to accurately perceive whether their neighbors are committed to conventional values if the neighborhood is characterized by residential mobility and a low socioeconomic status (Warner and Burchfield, 2011). Future research should investigate why this occurs.

Omitted Variable Bias

Another limitation of this study is the omission of contextual variables known to influence youth involvement in crime. By limiting the contextual variables examined in this study, the chances of omitted variable bias are increased. The current study examines neighborhood context and family context as control variables to explain youth involvement in crime. Neighborhood context (a macro-level construct) and families (a micro-level construct) are key predictors of behavior. However, schools and peers are additional contexts known to influence youth involvement in crime. Unlike the contextual variables examined in this study, schools and peers may not necessarily reflect the composition of a single neighborhood. Schools often enroll students from several neighborhoods and peers can be situated across a variety of neighborhoods. While the exclusion of these contexts may overestimate neighborhood effects (Cook, 2003; Duncan and Raudenbush, 2001; Elliott et al., 2006; Kirk, 2009), the significance of neighborhood effects examined in this study were limited,[4] a result which may lessen concerns regarding omitted variable bias to some extent.

School and peers are important contextual variables that can aid explanations of criminal behavior. They were not explored in the current study because the PHDCN data set does not contain information on school collective efficacy and data pertaining to peers are limited to youths' perceptions about other students' involvement in a variety of antisocial behaviors and socialization activities with peers. These constructs are not expected to influence orientation of locus of control or collective efficacy. Further, the PHDCN data could not be linked to additional data sets for the current study due to the limitations of the restricted data user's agreement with the Inter-University Consortium for Political and Social Research (ICPSR).

THEORETICAL IMPLICATIONS

The findings from this study evoke several theoretical implications; three of which are examined in this section. First, alternative theories may be responsible for the findings. Second, the influence of neighborhood contextual variables on the development of locus of control is relatively unexplored. Finally, youths' locus of control orientation (internal or external) may apply to antisocial behaviors as well as prosocial behaviors. These three theoretical implications are discussed in turn below.

Alternative Explanations of Crime

The current study examines the influence of locus of control on involvement in crime from a control perspective. As such, the major tenets of this study are: (1) youths have personal control over situations and their reactions to them, via an internal locus of control; and, (2) neighborhoods have the ability to enact control over their environment through collective efficacy. While this is the framework tested in this study, alternative theoretical explanations of youth involvement in crime are indeed feasible. Three such theoretical explanations are social learning, routine activities, and self-control.

Social learning theory in the fields of sociology and criminology is a well-established explanation of crime and delinquency (Akers, 1985; Akers and Jensen, 2006). Two learning theories, Sutherland's (1947) concept of differential association and Aker's (1985) social learning theory, support the hypothesis that antisocial behaviors are learned by the same mechanisms used in learning prosocial behaviors. Social learning theories in the field of social psychology also attempt to explain all behavior, not only criminal behavior. Arguably, the most well-known social learning theorist in psychology is Albert Bandura. However, fellow social psychologist Julian Rotter also developed a theory about behavior and learning. His social learning theory focuses on the relationships and interaction between an individual and his or her environment. Under Rotter's theory, there are four main factors influencing behavior: (1) behavior potential; (2) expectancy; (3) reinforcement value; and (4) psychological situation (Rotter, 1954; Lefcourt, 1976).

Locus of control was derived from Rotter's social learning theory and, therefore, it has been argued in this study that locus of control is influence by these four factors; particularly expectancy and reinforcement value. Expectancy and reinforcement value are essentially learned through life experiences and interactions with others and the environment. Expectancies are based on past experiences and allow people to develop a subjective expectation regarding the probability that a behavior will result in a particular outcome. Reinforcement value is the perceived desirability of the outcome associated with the behavior. Individuals also learn what is acceptable and how behaviors will be reinforced. Expectancies and reinforcement value are subjective and perceptions can vary based on an individual's prior history and experiences.

It is possible that instead of an internal locus of control influencing prosocial behavior (as is tested in this study), social learning better explains youth involvement in crime. Under social learning theory, youths may be differentially reinforced towards prosocial behavior and may have learned to expect certain outcomes to be a result of their actions. However, one important distinction between locus of control and social learning theory is the use of choice to explain behavior. It is anticipated that youths with an internal locus of control would be better equipped to choose alternatives to crime because they believe they have control over their life. The notion of choice in social learning theory, on the other hand, is subsumed under differential reinforcement (Akers, 1990). Accordingly, youths choose to engage in behaviors based on the anticipated rewards and punishments associated with that behavior and the mechanism or process by which youths choose alternatives to crime is not specifically addressed by social learning theory.

Routine activities theory is another potential theoretical explanation that supports the findings of the current research. According to routine activities theory, crime is more likely when there is a convergence of three specific elements: motivated offender, opportunity for the behavior, and an absence of capable guardians. Motivated offenders are considered to be constant and ubiquitous, and therefore researchers do not often test this component of the theory. The second element, opportunity, varies across individuals and is often called the root cause of crime (Felson, 2002). For example, if there are no vulnerable victims to attack and no one to whom to sell drugs, opportunity is lacking. The final element, absence of capable guardians, is also variable across individuals and situations. Capable guardians can take the form of either formal (e.g., police) or informal (e.g., primary caregiver, parent) social controls. Crime is less likely when a capable guardian is present because the guardian may intervene or call the police (e.g., collective efficacy) and they are a potential witness to the act who could later implicate the offender to formal and/or informal social controls. Absence of capable guardians works in tandem with opportunity. If the opportunity to engage in crime is present, and guardians who can prevent a criminal act are not present, crime is more likely to occur.

Again, as with social learning theory, routine activities theory does not explicate the mechanisms by which a youth chooses to engage in crime. Under routine activities theory, it is assumed that offenders rationally choose their activities as they would any other behavior. Routine activities theory, however, does not unpack how offenders make this choice.

Another potential explanation of crime is self-control. Self-control is consistently a significant predictor of crime and delinquency in criminological research (Pratt and Cullen, 2000), and differs from locus of control.[5] Self-control is conceptualized as a stable trait that is relatively set by age 8 (Gottfredson and Hirschi, 1990). Locus of control is also relatively stable (Reynolds, 1976) but can change through the accumulation of experiences related to expectancies and reinforcements over time (Lefcourt, 1982; Nowicki and Strickland, 1973). A key difference is that locus of control influences choices related to decisions and behavior whereas self-control does not consider agency or individual choice in decision making. Paternoster and

Pogarsky (2009: 110) aptly state: "Low self-control... is not a process of decision making or a way in which choices over alternative courses of action are made, indeed one low in self-control may be completely unaware that alternatives exist."[6] On the other hand, locus of control may facilitate decision making and whether individuals choose alternatives to crime.[7]

While social learning, routine activities, and self-control may aid in explaining youths' involvement in crime, the focus of the current study is on the use of an internal locus of control to guide prosocial behavior and facilitate choice. Locus of control is examined as a way of enacting personal control over situations and choosing alternatives to crime. The alternative explanations of crime reviewed above are unable to address the mechanisms associated with choice related to control over behavior and outcomes.

Influence of Contextual Variables on Locus of Control

Another theoretical implication stemming from this study is the need to determine whether context influences locus of control. In the current study, neighborhood and family context are examined as control variables and their direct effects on locus of control are not explored. Family context is known to influence children's locus of control orientation (Chance, 1965; Lefcourt, 1976), but what about neighborhood factors? Scholars postulate that the environment plays a role in the development of locus of control orientation through life history and learning experiences. However, research on which contexts are important is scant and criminological research in general lacks sufficient explanation for the mechanisms at work between neighborhoods and influence over individual behavior (see Taylor, 2010). Additional research could investigate the influence of contextual variables on locus of control orientation to determine if any are important in the development of locus of control. If found to play a significant role in the development of an internal locus of control, contextual variables could be targeted in the development of policies and programs aimed at assisting prosocial development of youth.

Locus of Control Perceptions and Antisocial Behaviors

While the locus of control measure in this study is interpreted as being prosocial, locus of control may address antisocial behavior. Theoretically, people can have an internal locus of control or an external locus of control about prosocial and antisocial behaviors. An internal locus of control could pertain to control over a desired outcome whether achieved through prosocial or problem behavior. In this study, an internal locus of control is significantly related to a reduction in crime. A locus of control instrument that encompasses problem behaviors may yield different results. The locus of control instrument used in this research, and those used in other studies, do not ask whether the respondent perceives outcomes related to involvement in crime to be under the control of the individual or a function of fate. Further, the locus of control measures used in this research may tap into antisocial behaviors, depending on the youths' interpretation of the questions. For example, "Can go far in the world" does not ask the youth to differentiate whether this would be achieved through legitimate or illegitimate means. Similarly, the question asking if youths' "Feel safe alone in neighborhood" does not determine if youths feel safe because they are comfortable deterring or fighting combatants as the need arises or if their neighborhood is generally safe (see Anderson, 1999).

POLICY IMPLICATIONS

Policy implications from this research stem from the finding that an internal locus of control is significantly related to a reduction in violence, drug dealing, and trouble with the police, independent of neighborhood. Most neighborhood context variables do not influence individual-level behavior in the current study of youth involvement in crime. This result is similar to that of Elliott and colleagues (2006) who found modest neighborhood effects on prosocial behavior. This finding is suggestive that it is more important to channel resources towards improving individuals' prosocial internal locus of control than to concentrate on developing a neighborhoods' collective efficacy. Further, programs aimed at developing an internal locus of control among youths may be useful in reducing antisocial behavior.

In order to encourage the development of an internal locus of control, first we need to know how it is developed. Rotter (1966) discusses how reinforcements and rewards are essential to behavior. Reinforcements and rewards are subjective probabilities – each person may interpret and react to them differently. Perceptions of reinforcements and rewards are developed according to one's locus of control orientation. Lefcourt (1982) underscores the influence of the environment in the development of locus of control (see also Twenge et al., 2004). This environment can include the family at the micro-level and communities and neighborhoods at the macro-level. Within these contexts, expectations for reinforcements and rewards will be developed based on the availability of prosocial role models that encourage responsibility for one's actions. Monitoring and socialization efforts also assist children in forming an internal locus of control (Chance, 1965; Lefcourt, 1976; Lynch et al., 2002; Phares, 1976).

Due to their importance in the development of an internal locus of control, increasing monitoring and socialization efforts among parents and other early childhood caregivers should be a focus of policymakers. Intervening early with parents and caregivers is essential because individuals are born without a sense of self. This sense of self is socially constructed (Bandura, 1997) and its development is based in early interactions with family and other primary caregivers (Bandura, 1997; Hoeltje et al., 1996). Further, as the principal agents of socialization and monitoring (see Bronfenbrenner, 1979), the family plays a key role in the development of a youth's internal locus of control (Lefcourt, 1976) and a lack of supervision and parental involvement with children is related to involvement in crime and delinquency (Loeber and Stouthamer-Loeber, 1986). Because of the importance of the family in developing locus of control orientations, early intervention programs aimed at socialization, monitoring, and increasing internal locus of control beliefs are ideal.

Several family-based prevention programs are effective and improve parenting skills such as monitoring and socialization and also have a positive effect on child outcomes (Farrington and Welsh, 2003; Piquero et al., 2009). Because locus of control development begins at an early age, a program which focuses on early developmental periods (i.e., pre-natal, infancy, and early childhood) is preferred. One such program is home visitation services provided by nurses to families at risk of child abuse and neglect. This program pairs nurses with at-risk pregnant women (e.g., young, low income, unmarried) during their first pregnancy. Nurses visit the mother nine times during the pregnancy and 23 times before the child's first birthday. During these visits, the nurse teaches the mother parenting self-efficacy and essential skills such as proper prenatal health behaviors (e.g., proper nutrition, avoiding drug and alcohol use) to reduce poor outcomes (e.g., pre-term birth, neurocognitive deficits), how to care for the child, and to plan for additional children.

In a randomized experiment of this home-visitation program, Olds and colleagues (1997, 1998) found long-term benefits among 400 women and their children over 15 years. Compared to women in the control group, who did not receive home visitation, women assigned to the program were less likely to abuse their child, have subsequent births, or require welfare assistance (e.g., Aid to Families with Dependent Children). Children of women assigned to the program were less likely to have behavioral problems resulting from drug and alcohol use by the mother and be arrested (self-report and official record) than children of mothers who were not enrolled in the home-visitation program.

These skills and the self-effectiveness they teach can translate into better parenting (e.g., socialization, monitoring), which in turn can influence the development of an internal locus of control in the child. Similarly, less intensive parenting classes for low-risk families who wish to increase their capabilities to socialize and monitor their children effectively would also aid the development of parental self-efficacy (see Elliott et al., 2006). It is believed that early intervention programs with parents of at-risk youth is one way to empower them to instill a sense of learned helpfulness in their children rather than learned helplessness which associated with an external locus of control (see Douglas and Bell, 2011). Additional research is needed to link the benefits of family-based prevention programs to offending behavior (see Farrington and Welsh, 2003). However, it is anticipated that these programs will increase the likelihood that children will develop an internal locus of control orientation which, according to the findings from the current study, should reduce involvement in crime.

Endnotes

Chapter 1

1. Although locus of control is often measured using omnibus scales, it is not an omnibus trait that universally relates to all aspects of life (see Lefcourt, 1976).
2. Sharkey uses part of the omnibus instrument examined in this study to investigate street efficacy.

Chapter 2

1. Sex offenders (N=42) did not differ from a community control group (N=42) on the locus of control measure. However, the number in each of these groups was small; thereby limiting generalizability.
2. Browning (2002) examines both rates and individual-level intimate partner violence.
3. Mediator models are more appropriate when the research question is whether an independent variable (e.g., locus of control) indirectly influences an outcome through another variable (e.g., collective efficacy).
4. Further, the PHDCN data set could not be linked to other data sources due to the limitations of the restricted data user's agreement with ICPSR and data available in the PHDCN publicly available data set do not provide informal social control measures on school and peers. Data on peers is limited to youths' perceptions about their peers' involvement in antisocial behavior.
5. These variables and constructs were chosen are based on the collective efficacy and criminological literature since more is

known about the effects of neighborhood context on collective efficacy and crime than locus of control.

6. This may depend on the quality of the relationships between the child and persons residing in the home. Family size could be a predictor of increased delinquency and crime. The current study is an exploratory analysis to determine if family size has an effect on locus of control and will not investigate the quality of family context. If there is a relationship, future research may seek to unravel why this might be the case.

Chapter 3

1. A second community survey was conducted in 2000. These data have not been made publicly available for analyses.

2. Ethnic heterogeneity is not available in the CS data set. It is obtained from the Wave 1 LCS data.

3. A total of 25 study participants died during the overall study data collection period. Sixteen died between Wave 1 and Wave 2, and 9 died between Wave 2 and Wave 3.

4. Wave 3 data are not the primary focus of this research and therefore the number of participants who moved between Wave 2 and Wave 3 is not addressed here.

5. Primary caregivers were not interviewed for Cohort 18 because many were legally adults. The mean age for these youths at Wave 1 was 18.14.

6. Individuals were not removed from the data set if they did not have data on the neighborhood context, family context, and/or individual-level control variables. Data reduction for these variables is handled during analyses that involve these variables.

7. Sharkey's scale includes two items (purposively damaged property and snatched purse) that are not typically considered violent offenses, and does not include two items that are violent offenses (robbery and sexual assault). The removal of purposively damaged property and snatched purse reduce the scale reliability to 0.03, and the inclusion of robbery and sexual assault reduce the scale reliability to 0.04. As part of his study on the relationship between low self-control and violent victimization using the PHDCN data, Gibson (2012)

examined involvement in violent crimes. In his violence scale, he did not include purposively damaged property and chased someone to scare; but did include hit someone you live with and use a weapon or force to get money or thing from people. The scale reliability coefficient using these twelve items is .653.

8. No one engaged in all 12 violent acts in the past 12 months.
9. Trouble with police is already a binary variable.
10. The bivariate relationships between self-reported involvement in crime at Wave 3 and locus of control at Wave 2 are examined later in this chapter.
11. A factor analysis was also conducted to force-fit one factor. The factor loadings did not change.
12. No rotation method was employed because only 1 component was extracted.
13. The chi-square tests used locus of control data from Cohorts 9 and 12 at Wave 2 and Wave 3; locus of control data are not available for Cohort 15 at Wave 3.
14. The last two items were reverse coded before they were added to the original PHDCN data set.
15. However, primary caregivers and youths in Cohort 18 were asked about their perceptions of collective efficacy during Wave 3 of the study.
16. This may imply a weak relationship between neighborhood context and family context variables.
17. This variable is not available for use by those with a restricted data user's agreement or the general public.
18. The question "When did you come to live in the USA?" was only asked of people answering that they were born outside of the United States.
19. Due to potential temporal ordering issues, bivariate relationships between the outcomes at Wave 3 and locus of control at Wave 2 are also examined. The bivariate relationship between violence at Wave 3 and locus of control at Wave 2 is -0.203 ($p = 0.002$). For a standard deviation increase in locus of control at Wave 2, involvement in violence at Wave 3 is expected to decrease by 17.19%.

20. The bivariate relationship between drug dealing at Wave 3 and locus of control at Wave 2 is -0.154 ($p = 0.296$). Although not statistically significant, the negative relationship identified when examining both variables at Wave 2 holds when considering temporal ordering. For a standard deviation increase in locus of control at Wave 2, involvement in drug dealing at Wave 3 is expected to decrease by 13.33%.

21. The bivariate relationship between trouble with police at Wave 3 and locus of control at Wave 2 is -0.183 ($p = 0.004$). For a standard deviation increase in locus of control at Wave 2, trouble with the police at Wave 3 is expected to decrease by 15.63%.

22. The models shown are the standard HLM models. During analyses, a hierarchical generalized linear model (HGLM) is used because the outcome variables follow a Poisson (i.e., violent crime and drug dealing scales) and logistic distribution (i.e., trouble with police), respectively.

23. The models allowing the intercept and slope error terms to vary were also employed. The chi-square tests were not significant for drug dealing and trouble with police indicating that the error terms should be fixed. For all models, the overall results did not change when error terms were allowed to vary (those results are not reported here).

24. There are no error terms in binary outcome variables; the variance is a function of the mean (Luke, 2004).

25. Models using the raw metric (not centering) and grand-mean centering are equivalent (Kreft, de Leeuw, and Aiken, 1995).

26. Models for the drug dealing scale and trouble with police are omitted and only one full mixed-effects model is shown for Model 2b.

27. Models for the drug dealing scale and trouble with police are omitted and only one full mixed-effects model is shown for Model 3c.

Chapter 4

1. Some neighborhoods do not have any youths involved in the criminal behaviors measured in this study. Those neighborhoods are included in the figure, but are represented by blank bars because there is no data to report.

2. Similar models were employed to examine the relationship between locus of control at Wave 2 and crime at Wave 3. The intercept coefficients for these models are -0.61 ($p < 0.000$; violence), -3.08 ($p < 0.000$; drug dealing), and -1.09 ($p < 0.000$; trouble with police).

3. For Wave 3 crime outcomes, each unit increase in locus of control decreases expected involvement in violence by a factor of 0.83 ($p < 0.001$) and decreases the odds of being in trouble with police by 0.83 ($p < 0.01$). The influence of locus of control at Wave 2 does not significantly influence drug dealing at Wave 3 ($\beta = -0.168; p > 0.05$).

4. Percent change was calculated using the formula: $100*\{exp(\beta *\delta)-1\}$, where δ equals 0.929.

5. The intercept coefficients for the models examining the outcomes at Wave 3 are -0.63 ($p < 0.000$; violence), -3.05 ($p < 0.000$; drug dealing), and -1.10 ($p < 0.01$; trouble with police).

6. For Wave 3 crime outcomes, each unit increase in locus of control decreases expected involvement in violence by a factor of 0.81 ($p < 0.000$), drug dealing by a factor of 0.59 ($p < 0.05$), and decreases the odds of being in trouble with police by 0.80 ($p < 0.01$).

7. Model 1c and Model 1d build on Model 1a instead of Model 1b because there do not appear to be any significant differences in locus of control between neighborhoods. Consequently, the slope error terms in Model 1c and Model 1d mimic Model 1a and are fixed.

8. Cohort 9 was chosen as the reference group based on the negative bivariate relationship between Cohort 9 and the outcome variables.

9. The percent change in drug dealing for Cohort 15 compared to Cohort 9 is unexpectedly large. The data available for the drug dealing measure is sparse which may affect the estimates. Few youths reported involvement in drug dealing (N = 58;

marijuana; N = 22; crack/cocaine; N = 3; heroin) and the behavior is concentrated in a small number of neighborhoods (N = 39).

10. In comparing the results from Models 1a and 1b, it was determined that the influence of locus of control on the outcomes did not vary by neighborhood.

11. Similar results were obtained using models where the error terms were allowed to vary (data not shown). One difference between these two models is the gamma value (γ_{10}) for the locus of control slope (β_1) for the drug dealing outcome. This value is -1.837 ($p = 0.072$) in the model with fixed error terms and -1.004 ($p = 0.208$) in the model with random error terms.

Chapter 5

1. Concentrated disadvantage is measured using the following variables from 1990 census data: percentage of poor families, percentage of single-parent families, percentage of families receiving welfare, and unemployment rate.

2. In cases of moderation, it is expected that the relationship between the independent variable (i.e., locus of control) and dependent variables (i.e., violence, drug dealing, and trouble with police) will change direction and/or strength after a moderator variable (i.e., collective efficacy) is added to the model (see Baron and Kenny, 1986).

3. Figure 5 displays the mean involvement in drug dealing by neighborhood cluster and reveals that drug dealing is limited to 39 neighborhood clusters (compared to violence and trouble with police which are reported in 75 and 72 neighborhood clusters, respectively). Further, the intra-class correlation indicates a clustering effect where neighborhood explains 23% of the variance related to involvement in drug dealing.

4. Neighborhood SES is significantly related to violence (Models 1d and 3c), drug dealing (Model 1d), and trouble with police (Model 3c); neighborhood ethnic heterogeneity is significantly related to drug dealing (Models 1d and 3c); and collective efficacy is significantly related to trouble with police (Model 3c). The other neighborhood level variables (residential

mobility and family disruption) are not related to the outcomes in any of the models.

5. While conceptually different, their origins are similar. Like locus of control, self-control is considered to be a function of parental monitoring and socialization (Gottfredson and Hirschi, 1990).

6. It is not clear whether the opposite is true; if high self-control can contribute to decision making. Preliminary results indicate that neighborhood contexts may influence locus of control.

7. Future research on criminal decision-making and choice may also consider examining thoughtfully reflective decision-making which accounts for changes in decision-making over time and contextual influence on choice (Paternoster and Pogarsky, 2009; Paternoster, Pogarsky, and Zimmerman, 2011) and affective states that can impact self-control and decision-making (see Van Gelder and De Vries, 2012).

Appendix

Table 1A. Correlation Matrix for Locus of Control and Family Context Variables

	Locus of Control	Immigrant Status	SES	Family Disruption	Family Size	Parental Monitoring
Locus of Control	1.000					
Immigrant Status	-0.081	1.000				
SES	0.156	-0.342	1.000			
Family Disruption	-0.031	-0.159	-0.072	1.000		
Family Size	-0.056	0.153	-0.218	-0.164	1.000	
Parental Monitoring	0.125	-0.069	0.116	-0.049	-0.030	1.000

Table 2A. Correlation Matrix for Locus of Control and Individual-Level Variables

	Locus of Control	Cohort 9	Cohort 12	Cohort 15	Male	African American	Hispanic
Locus of Control	1.000						
Cohort 9	0.051	1.000					
Cohort 12	0.033	-0.546	1.000				
Cohort 15	-0.089	-0.467	-0.486	1.000			
Male	-0.051	0.069	-0.023	-0.047	1.000		
African American	0.041	-0.018	0.023	-0.006	-0.034	1.000	
Hispanic	-0.116	0.022	-0.019	-0.002	0.019	-0.572	1.000

Table 3A. Correlation matrix for 23 locus of control items

	1	2	3	4	5	6	7
1	1.000						
2	0.164	1.000					
3	0.182	0.374	1.000				
4	0.209	0.191	0.191	1.000			
5	0.176	0.305	0.398	0.156	1.000		
6	0.203	0.209	0.275	0.317	0.261	1.000	
7	0.218	0.227	0.233	0.279	0.294	0.413	1.000
8	0.058	0.176	0.228	0.084	0.260	0.116	0.159
9	0.154	0.177	0.152	0.198	0.172	0.228	0.254
10	0.163	0.152	0.179	0.231	0.217	0.320	0.336
11	0.157	0.129	0.175	0.215	0.179	0.234	0.284
12	0.148	0.141	0.142	0.163	0.098	0.231	0.273
13	0.149	0.183	0.203	0.214	0.235	0.291	0.350
14	0.128	0.074	0.099	0.178	0.091	0.116	0.160
15	0.225	0.178	0.217	0.280	0.280	0.349	0.385
16	0.179	0.182	0.205	0.275	0.251	0.289	0.399
17	0.066	0.200	0.232	0.104	0.302	0.168	0.222
18	0.129	0.138	0.138	0.179	0.117	0.160	0.197
19	0.104	0.185	0.252	0.157	0.223	0.166	0.188
20	0.068	0.128	0.200	0.155	0.203	0.197	0.195
21	0.085	0.039	0.056	0.169	0.045	0.159	0.155
22	0.108	0.072	0.057	0.192	0.039	0.165	0.195
23	0.065	0.155	0.155	0.160	0.148	0.110	0.135

Table 3A, continued. Correlation matrix for 23 locus of control
items

	8	9	10	11	12	13	14
8	1.000						
9	0.302	1.000					
10	0.248	0.360	1.000				
11	0.313	0.406	0.403	1.000			
12	0.113	0.273	0.278	0.333	1.000		
13	0.314	0.384	0.419	0.462	0.331	1.000	
14	-0.009	0.132	0.135	0.117	0.143	0.091	1.000
15	0.101	0.244	0.352	0.221	0.192	0.283	0.202
16	0.113	0.239	0.231	0.167	0.192	0.256	0.192
17	0.157	0.162	0.210	0.151	0.147	0.215	0.116
18	0.062	0.177	0.157	0.166	0.204	0.184	0.170
19	0.161	0.156	0.195	0.162	0.148	0.206	0.102
20	0.122	0.135	0.185	0.107	0.120	0.187	0.115
21	-0.001	0.120	0.131	0.082	0.168	0.110	0.204
22	-0.018	0.115	0.147	0.121	0.194	0.142	0.182
23	0.115	0.142	0.121	0.144	0.125	0.168	0.067

	15	16	17	18	19	20	21
15	1.000						
16	0.363	1.000					
17	0.251	0.249	1.000				
18	0.178	0.186	0.133	1.000			
19	0.219	0.202	0.167	0.178	1.000		
20	0.212	0.185	0.188	0.184	0.277	1.000	
21	0.139	0.191	0.078	0.227	0.129	0.235	1.000
22	0.140	0.199	0.060	0.288	0.182	0.183	0.435
23	0.100	0.158	0.256	0.125	0.282	0.192	0.077

	22	23
22	1.000	
23	0.100	1.000

Table 4A. Correlation matrix for locus of control, collective efficacy, neighborhood context, and family context variables

| | Locus of Control | Collective Efficacy | NEIGHBORHOOD | | | | FAMILY | | | | |
			Residential Mobility	SES	Ethnic Heterogeneity	Residential Mobility	Immigrant Status	SES	Family Disruption	Family Size	Parental Monitoring
Locus of Control	1.000										
Collective Efficacy	0.067	1.000									
NEIGHBORHOOD Residential Mobility	-0.035	-0.479	1.000								
SES	0.111	0.658	-0.229	1.000							
Ethnic Heterogeneity	-0.049	-0.236	0.448	-0.108	1.000						
Residential Mobility	-0.013	-0.231	-0.018	-0.226	-0.069	1.000					

Table 4A, continued. Correlation matrix for locus of control, collective efficacy, neighborhood context, and family context variables

	Locus of Control	Collective Efficacy	NEIGHBORHOOD				FAMILY				
			Residential Mobility	SES	Ethnic Heterogeneity	Residential Mobility	Immigrant Status	SES	Family Disruption	Family Size	Parental Monitoring
FAMILY											
Immigrant Status	-0.081	-0.239	0.248	-0.110	0.246	-0.207	1.000				
SES	0.156	0.349	-0.144	0.402	-0.128	-0.021	-0.342	1.000			
Family Disruption	-0.031	0.004	-0.025	-0.003	-0.049	0.062	-0.158	-0.072	1.000		
Family Size	-0.056	-0.128	-0.002	-0.154	0.016	-0.008	0.153	-0.218	-0.164	1.000	
Parental Monitoring	0.125	-0.008	-0.024	-0.007	0.016	0.040	-0.069	0.116	-0.049	-0.030	1.000

Table 5A. Home Inventory

1.	Subject has a set time [curfew] to be home on school nights.	A. Yes B. No
2.	Subject routinely obeys curfew on school nights.	A. Yes B. No
3.	Subject has a set time [curfew] to be home on weekend nights.	A. Yes B. No
4.	Subject routinely obeys curfew on weekend nights.	A. Yes B. No
5.	PC has established rules about homework and checks to see if homework is done.	A. Yes B. No
6.	PC assisted subject with homework and school assignments every other week during current or most recent school year.	A. Yes B. No
7.	PC requires subject to sleep at home on school nights.	A. Yes B. No
8.	When PC is not available to subject at home, reasonable procedures have been established for him/her to check in with PC, or their designee, on weekends and after school.	A. Yes B. No
9.	After school subject goes somewhere that adult supervision is provided.	A. Yes B. No
10.	PC establishes rules for subject's behavior with peers and asks questions to determine whether they are being followed.	A. Yes B. No
11.	Subject is not allowed to wander in public places without adult supervision for more than 1 hour *(Cohort 9)*/2 hours *(Cohort 12)*/3 hours *(Cohort 15)*.	A. Yes B. No
12.	PC has had contact with two of the subjects' friends in the last week *(Cohort 9)*/two weeks *(Cohorts 12 and 15)*.	A. Yes B. No

Table 5A, continued. Home Inventory

13. PC talks daily with subject about his/her day.	A. Yes B. No
14. PC has visited school or talked to the teacher or counselor <u>within the last 3 months.</u>	A. Yes B. No
15. Family has TV, and it is used judiciously, not left on continuously.	A. Yes B. No
16. PC has discussed television programs with subject <u>during the past two weeks.</u>	A. Yes B. No
17. PC has discussed current events with subject <u>during the past two weeks.</u>	A. Yes B. No
18 PC has discussed the hazards of alcohol and drug abuse with subject <u>during the past year.</u>	A. Yes B. No
19. PC denies subject access to alcohol (including beer or wine) in the home.	A. Yes B. No
20. PC knows signs of drug usage and remains alert to possible experimentation.	A. Yes B. No
21. Subject is taken regularly to a doctor's office or clinic for check-ups and preventive health care (<u>once a year</u>).	A. Yes B. No
22. Family has a fairly regular and predictable schedule for subject.	A. Yes B. No
23. PC sets limits for subject and generally enforces them.	A. Yes B. No
24. PC is generally consistent in establishing or applying family rules.	A. Yes B. No

References

Agnew, Robert, and Helene Raskin White. 1992. An Empirical Test of General Strain Theory. *Criminology* 30:475-499.

Akers, Ronald L. 1985. *Deviant Behavior: A Social Learning Approach.* Belmont, CA: Wadsworth.

Akers, Ronald L. 1990. Rational Choice, Deterrence, and Social Learning in Criminology: The Path Not Taken. *The Journal of Criminal Law & Criminology* 81:653-676.

Akers, Ronald L., and Gary F. Jensen. 2006. The Empirical Status of Social Learning Theory of Crime and Deviance: The Past, Present, and Future. Pp. 37-76 in *Taking Stock: The Status of Criminological Theory, Advances in Criminological Theory, Volume 15.* eds. Francis T. Cullen, John Paul Wright, and Kristie R. Blevins. New Brunswick, NJ: Transaction.

Anderson, Elijah. 1999. *Code of the Street.* New York: W.W. Norton and Company.

Bandura, Albert. 1986. Self-Efficacy. Pp. 390-453 in *Social Foundations of Thought and Action: A Social Cognitive Theory.* Englewood Cliffs, NJ: Prentice-Hall.

Bandura, Albert. 1997. *Self-Efficacy: The Exercise of Control.* New York: Freeman and Company.

Bandura, Albert. 2000. Exercise of Human Agency Through Collective Efficacy. *Current Directions in Psychological Science* 9:75-78.

Baron, Reuben M., and David A. Kenny. 1986. The Moderator-Mediator Variable Distinction in Social Psychological Research: Conceptual, Strategic, and Statistical Considerations. *Journal of Personality and Social Psychology* 51:1173-1182.

Battle, Esther S., and Julian B. Rotter. 1963. Children's Feelings of Personal Control as Related to Social Class and Ethnic Group. *Journal of Personality* 31:482-490.

Biggs, S.J., M.P. Bender, and J. Foreman. 1983. Are There Psychological Differences Between Persistent Solvent-Abusing Delinquents and Delinquents Who Do Not Abuse Solvents? *Journal of Adolescence* 6:71-86.

Blake, Susan M., Rebecca Ledsky, Carol Goodenow, and Lydia O'Donnell. 2001. Recency of Immigration, Substance Use, and Sexual Behavior Among Massachusetts Adolescents. *American Journal of Public Health* 91:794-798.

Bowen, Erica, and Elizabeth Gilchrist. 2006. Predicting Dropout of Court-Mandated Treatment in a British Sample of Domestic Violence Offenders. *Psychology, Crime & Law* 12:573-587.

Bradley, Robert H., Robert F. Corwyn, Bettye M. Caldwell, Leanne Whiteside-Mansell, Gail A. Wasserman, and Iris T. Mink. 2000. Measuring the Home Environments of Children in Early Adolescence. *Journal of Research on Adolescence* 10:247-288.

Brody, Gene H., Xiaojia Ge, Rand D. Conger, Frederick X. Gibbons, Velma McBride Murry, Meg Gerrard, and Ronald L. Simons. 2001. The Influence of Neighborhood Disadvantage, Collective Socialization, and Parenting on African American Children's Affiliation with Deviant Peers. *Child Development* 72:1231–1246.

Bronfenbrenner, Urie. 1979. *The Ecology of Human Development: Experiments by Nature and Design.* Cambridge, MA: Harvard University Press.

Bronfenbrenner, Urie. 1986a. Ecology of the Family as a Context for Human Development: Research Perspectives. *Developmental Psychology* 22:723-742.

Bronfenbrenner, Urie. 1986b. Recent Advances in Research on the Ecology of Human Development. Pp. 285-309 in *Development as Action in Context: Problem Behavior and Normal Youth Development.* eds. Rainer K. Silbereisen, Klaus Eyferth, and Georg Rudinger. New York: Springer-Verlag.

Bronfenbrenner, Urie. 1992. Ecological Systems Theory. Pp. 187-249 in *Six Theories of Child Development: Revised Formulations and*

Current Issues. ed. Ross Vasta. Philadelphia, PA: Jessica Kingsley Publishers.

Brooks-Gunn, Jeanne, Greg J. Duncan, and J. Lawrence Aber. 1997a. *Neighborhood Poverty: Context and Consequences for Children, Volume 1.* New York: Russell Sage Foundation.

Brooks-Gunn, Jeanne, Greg J. Duncan, and J. Lawrence Aber. 1997b. *Neighborhood Poverty: Policy Implications in Studying Neighborhoods, Volume 2.* New York: Russell Sage Foundation.

Brooks-Gunn, Jeanne, Greg J. Duncan, Pamela Kato Klebanov, and Naomi Sealand. 1993. Do Neighborhoods Influence Child and Adolescent Development? *American Journal of Sociology* 99:353-395.

Browning, Christopher R. 2002. The Span of Collective Efficacy: Extending Social Disorganization Theory to Partner Violence. *Journal of Marriage and Family* 64:833-850.

Browning, Christopher R., and Kathleen A. Cagney. 2003. Moving Beyond Poverty: Neighborhood Structure, Social Processes, and Health. *Journal of Health and Social Behavior* 44:552-571.

Browning, Christopher R., Tama Leventhal, and Jeanne Brooks-Gunn. 2004. Neighborhood Context and Racial Differences in Early Adolescent Sexual Activity. *Demography* 41:697-720.

Bursik, Krisanne, and Timothy A. Martin. 2006. Ego Development and Adolescent Academic Achievement. *Journal of Research on Adolescence* 16:1-18.

Bursik, Robert J., Jr. 1986. Ecological Stability and the Dynamics of Delinquency. Pp. 35-66 in *Communities and Crime.* eds. Albert J. Reiss and Michael H. Tonry. Chicago, IL: Chicago University Press.

Bursik, Robert J., Jr. 1988. Social Disorganization and Theories of Crime and Delinquency: Problems and Prospects. *Criminology* 26:519-551.

Bursik, Robert J., Jr., and Harold G. Grasmick. 1993. *Neighborhoods and Crime: The Dimensions of Effective Community Control.* New York: Lexington Books.

Burton, Linda M., and Robin L. Jarrett. 2000. In the Mix, Yet on the Margins: The Place of Families in Urban Neighborhood and Child

Development Research. *Journal of Marriage and the Family* 62:1114-1135.

Byrne, James M., and Robert J. Sampson. 1986. Key Issues in the Social Ecology of Crime. Pp. 1-22 in *The Social Ecology of Crime.* eds. James M. Byrne and Robert J. Sampson. New York: Springer-Verlag.

Caldwell, Bettye, and Robert H. Bradley. 1984. *Home Observation for Measurement of the Environment (HOME) - Revised Edition.* Little Rock, AR: University of Arkansas.

Caputo, Alicia A., and Stanley L. Brodsky. 2004. Citizen Coping with Community Notification of Released Sex Offenders. *Behavioral Sciences and the Law* 22:239-252.

Chance, June E. 1965. Internal Control of Reinforcements and the School Learning Process. *Paper Presented at the Society for Research in Child Development Convention,* Minneapolis, MN.

Cloward, Richard A., and Lloyd E. Ohlin. 1960. *Delinquency and Opportunity.* New York: Free Press.

Cole, Ester, and Claire Ivy Gayle Kumchy. 1981. The CIP Battery: Identification of Depression in a Juvenile Delinquent Population. *Journal of Clinical Psychology* 18:880-884.

Coleman, James S. 1990. *Foundations of Social Theory.* Cambridge, MA: Belknap Press.

Cook, Thomas D. 2003. The Case for Studying Multiple Contexts Simultaneously. *Addiction* 98:151-155.

Cook, Thomas D., Melissa R. Herman, Meredith Phillips, and Richard A. Settersten, Jr. 2002. Some Ways in Which Neighborhoods, Nuclear Families, Friendship Groups, and Schools Jointly Affect Early Adolescent Development. *Child Development* 73:1283-1309.

Cross, Herbert J., and James J. Tracy. 1971. Personality Factors in Delinquent Boys: Differences Between Blacks and Whites. *Journal of Research in Crime and Delinquency* 8:10-22.

Dalgard, Odd Stefen, Suraj Bahadur Thapa, Edvard Hauff, Michael McCubbin, and Hammad Raza Syed. 2006. Immigration, Lack of Control and Psychological Distress: Findings from the Oslo Health Study. *Scandinavian Journal of Psychology* 47:551-558.

Dekel, Rachel, Rami Benbenishty, and Yair Amram. 2004. Therapeutic Communities for Drug Addicts: Prediction of Long-Term Outcomes. *Addictive Behaviors* 29:1833-1837.

Douglas, Kobie, and Carl C. Bell. 2011. Youth Homicide Prevention. *Psychiatric Clinics of North America* 34:205-216.

Duke, Marshall P., and Eulalie Fenhagen. 1975. Self-Parental Alienation and Locus of Control in Delinquent Girls. *The Journal of Genetic Psychology* 127:103-107.

Duncan, David F. 1996. Growing Up Under the Gun: Children and Adolescents Coping with Violent Neighborhoods. *The Journal of Primary Prevention* 16:343-356.

Duncan, Greg J., and J. Lawrence Aber. 1997. Neighborhood Models and Measures. Pp. 62-78 in *Neighborhood Poverty: Context and Consequences for Children, Volume 1.* eds. Jeanne Brooks-Gunn, Greg J. Duncan, and J. Lawrence Aber. New York: Russell Sage Foundation.

Duncan, Greg J., Jeanne Brooks-Gunn, and Pamela K. Klebanov. 1994. Economic Deprivation and Early-Childhood Development. *Child Development* 65:296-318.

Duncan, Greg J., and Stephen W. Raudenbush. 1999. Assessing the Effects of Context in Studies of Child and Youth Development. *Educational Psychologist* 34:29-41.

Duncan, Greg J., and Stephen W. Raudenbush. 2001. Neighborhoods and Adolescent Development: How Can We Determine the Links? Pp. 105-136 in *Does It Take a Village? Community Effects on Children, Adolescents and Families.* eds. Alan Booth and Ann C. Crouter. Mahwah, NJ: Lawrence Erlbaum Associates.

Efta-Breitbach, Jill, and Kurt A. Freeman. 2004. Recidivism, Resilience, and Treatment Effectiveness for Youth Who Sexually Offend. *Journal of Child Sexual Abuse* 13:257-279.

Elder, Glen H., Jr. 1994. Time, Human Agency, and Social Change: Perspectives on the Life Course. *Social Psychology Quarterly* 57:4-15.

Elder, Glen H., Jr. 1995. Life Trajectories in Changing Societies. Pp. 46-68 in *Self-Efficacy in Changing Societies.* ed. Albert Bandura. Cambridge, UK: Cambridge University Press.

Elliott, Delbert S., Scott Menard, Bruce Rankin, Amanda Elliott, William Julius Wilson, and David Huizinga. 2006. *Good Kids from Bad Neighborhoods: Successful Development in Social Context.* Cambridge, UK: Cambridge University Press.

Fabio, Anthony, Li-Chuan Tu, Rolf Loeber, and Jacqueline Cohen. 2011. Neighborhood Socioeconomic Disadvantage and the Shape of the Age-Crime Curve. *American Journal of Public Health* 101:S325-S332.

Farrington, David P. 1986. Age and Crime. Pp. 189-250 in *Crime and Justice: A Review of Research, Volume 7.* eds. Michael H. Tonry and Norval Morris. Chicago, IL: University of Chicago Press.

Farrington, David P. 1992. Explaining the Beginning, Progress and Ending of Antisocial Behavior from Birth to Adulthood. Pp. 253-286 in *Facts, Frameworks and Forecasts, Advances in Criminological Theory, Volume 3.* ed. Joan McCord. New Brunswick, NJ: Transaction.

Farrington, David P. 1993. Have any Individual, Family or Neighbourhood Influences on Offending been Demonstrated Conclusively? Pp. 7-37 in *Integrating Individual and Ecological Aspects of Crime.* eds. David P. Farrington, Robert J. Sampson, and Per-Olof H. Wikström. Stockholm, Sweden: National Council for Crime Prevention.

Farrington, David P. 1995. The Development of Offending and Antisocial Behaviour from Childhood: Key Findings from the Cambridge Study in Delinquent Development. *Journal of Child Psychology and Psychiatry* 360:929-964.

Farrington, David P. 2003. Developmental and Life-Course Criminology: Key Theoretical and Empirical Issues - The 2002 Sutherland Award Address. *Criminology* 41:221-255.

Farrington, David P., and Brandon C. Welsh. 2003. Family-Based Prevention of Offending: A Meta-Analysis. *The Australian and New Zealand Journal of Criminology* 36:127-151.

Felson, Marcus. 2002. *Crime and Everyday Life.* Thousand Oaks, CA: Sage.

Fernández-Ballesteros, Rocio, Juan Díez-Nicolás, Gian Vittorio Caprara, Claudio Barbaranelli, and Albert Bandura. 2002.

Determinants and Structural Relation of Personal Efficacy to Collective Efficacy. *Applied Psychology: An International Review* 51:107-125.

Findley, Maureen J., and Harris M. Cooper. 1983. Locus of Control and Academic Achievement: A Literature Review. *Journal of Personality and Social Psychology* 44: 419-427.

Foglia, Wanda D. 2000. Adding an Explicit Focus on Cognition to Criminological Theory. Pp.10-1 – 10-25 in *The Science, Treatment, and Prevention of Antisocial Behaviors: Application to the Criminal Justice System.* ed. Diana H. Fishbein. Kingston, NJ: Civic Research Institute.

Fraser, Mark W. 1996. Aggressive Behavior in Childhood and Early Adolescence: An Ecological-Developmental Perspective on Youth Violence. *Social Work* 41:347-361.

Frytak, Jennifer R., Carolyn R. Harley, and Michael D. Finch. 2003. Socioeconomic Status and Health Over the Life Course: Capital as a Unifying Concept. Pp. 623-643 in *Handbook of the Life Course.* eds. Jeylan T. Mortimer and Michael J. Shanahan. New York: Kluwer Academic/Plenum Publishers.

Furstenberg, Frank F., Jr., Thomas D. Cook, Jacquelynne Eccles, Glen H. Elder, Jr., and Arnold Sameroff. 1999. *Managing to Make It: Urban Families and Adolescent Success.* Chicago, IL: University of Chicago Press.

Gephart, Martha A. 1997. Neighborhoods and Communities as Contexts for Development. Pp. 120-131 in *Neighborhood Poverty: Context and Consequences for Children, Volume 1.* eds. Jeanne Brooks-Gunn, Greg J. Duncan, and J. Lawrence Aber. New York: Russell Sage Foundation.

Gibson, Chris L. 2012. *Unpacking the Influence of Neighborhood Context and Antisocial Propensity on Violent Victimization of Children and Adolescents in Chicago.* Washington, DC: Department of Justice.

Gierowski, Józef K., and Tomasz Rajtar. 2003. Chosen Factors Influencing the Locus of Control in Perpetrators of Criminal Acts. *Problems of Forensic Science* LIII:129-138.

Gorman-Smith, Deborah, Patrick H. Tolan, and David B. Henry. 2000. A Developmental-Ecological Model of the Relation of Family Functioning to Patterns of Delinquency. *Journal of Quantitative Criminology* 16:169-198.

Gorman-Smith, Deborah, Patrick H. Tolan, Arnaldo Zelli, and L. Rowell Huesmann. 1996. The Relation of Family Functioning to Violence Among Inner-City Minority Youths. *Journal of Family Psychology* 10:115-129.

Gottfredson, Michael R., and Travis Hirschi. 1990. *A General Theory of Crime*. Stanford, CA: Stanford University Press.

Gottfredson, Michael R., and Travis Hirschi. 2003. Self-Control and Opportunity. Pp. 5-20 in *Control Theories of Crime and Delinquency, Advances in Criminological Theory, Volume 12*. eds. Chester L. Britt and Michael R. Gottfredson. New Brunswick, NJ: Transaction Publishers.

Graffeo, Lisa Cotlar, and Lynett Silvestri. 2006. Relationships Between Locus of Control and Health-Related Variables. *Education* 126: 593-596.

Graham, Kevin R. 1993. Toward a Better Understanding and Treatment of Sex Offenders. *International Journal of Offender Therapy and Comparative Criminology* 37:41-57.

Griffith, James E., Amelia Pennington-Averett, and Inez Bryan. 1981. Women Prisoners' Multidimensional Locus of Control. *Criminal Justice and Behavior* 8:375-389.

Groh, Thomas R., and Edward E. Goldenberg. 1976. Locus of Control Within Subgroups in a Correctional Population. *Criminal Justice and Behavior* 39:169-178.

Hains, Anthony A., and Leo P. Herrman. 1989. Social Cognitive Skills and Behavioural Adjustment of Delinquent Adolescents in Treatment. *Journal of Adolescence* 12:323-328.

Halloran, Elizabeth C., Diana M. Doumas, Richard S. John, and Gayla Margolin. 1999. The Relationship Between Aggression in Children and Locus of Control Beliefs. *The Journal of Genetic Psychology* 160:5-21.

Haynie, Dana L. 2002. Friendship Networks and Delinquency: The Relative Nature of Peer Delinquency. *Journal of Quantitative Criminology* 18:99-134.

Heimer, Karen. 2000. Changes in the Gender Gap in Crime and Women's Economic Marginalization. Pp. 427-484 in *The Nature of Crime: Continuity and Change, Criminal Justice 2000, Volume 1*. ed. Gary LaFree. Washington, DC: U.S. Department of Justice.

Hersch, Paul D., and Karl E. Scheibe. 1967. Reliability and Validity of Internal-External Control as a Personality Dimension. *Journal of Consulting Psychology* 31:609-613.

Hindelang, Michael J., Travis Hirschi, and Joseph G. Weis. 1979. Correlates of Delinquency: The Illusion of Discrepancy between Self-Report and Official Measures. *American Sociological Review* 44:995-1014.

Hindelang, Michael J., Travis Hirschi, and Joseph G. Weis. 1981. *Measuring Delinquency*. Beverly Hills, CA: Sage.

Hirschi, Travis, and Michael R. Gottfredson. 1983. Age and the Explanation of Crime. *American Journal of Sociology* 89:552-584.

Hirschi, Travis, and Michael R. Gottfredson. 2001. Self-Control Theory. Pp. 81-96 in *Explaining Criminals and Crime: Essays in Contemporary Criminological Theory*. eds. Raymond Paternoster and Ronet Bachman. Los Angeles, CA: Roxbury.

Hitlin, Steven, and Glen H. Elder, Jr. 2007. Time, Self, and the Curiously Abstract Concept of Agency. *Sociological Theory* 25:170-191.

Hoeltje, Claudia O., Stephen R. Zubrick, Sven R. Silburn, and Alison F. Garton. 1996. Generalized Self-Efficacy: Family and Adjustment Correlates. *Journal of Clinical Child Psychology* 25:446-453.

Hollin, Clive R. 1989. *Psychology and Crime*. New York, NY: Routledge.

Houts, Sandra, and Cathy Kassab. 1997. Rotter's Social Learning Theory and Fear of Crime: Differences by Race and Ethnicity. *Social Science Quarterly* 78:122-136.

Inter-University Consortium for Political and Social Research, Project on Human Development in Chicago Neighborhoods Website.

http://www.icpsr.umich.edu/PHDCN/site-selection.html. Date
Accessed: January 4, 2009.

Jerusalem, Matthias, and Waldemar Mittag. 1995. Self-Efficacy in
Stressful Life Transitions. Pp. 177-201 in *Self-Efficacy in Changing
Societies.* ed. Albert Bandura. Cambridge, UK: Cambridge
University Press.

Jerusalem, Matthias, and Ralf Schwarzer. 1992. Self-Efficacy as a
Resource Factor in Stress Appraisal Processes. Pp. 195-213 in *Self-
Efficacy: Thought Control of Action.* ed. Ralf Schwarzer.
Philadephia, PA: Hemisphere Publishing Corporation.

Juby, Heather, and David P. Farrington. 2001. Disentangling the Link
Between Disrupted Families and Delinquency. *British Journal of
Criminology* 41:22-40.

Junger, Marianne, and Maja Deković. 2003. Crime as Risk-Taking: Co-
Occurrence of Delinquent Behavior, Health Endangering Behaviors
and Problem Behaviors. Pp. 213-248 in *Control Theories of Crime
and Delinquency, Advances in Criminological Theory.* eds. Chester
L. Britt and Michael R. Gottfredson. New Brunswick NJ:
Transaction Publisher.

Karabenick, Stuart A., and Thomas K. Srull. 1978. Effects of
Personality and Situational Variation in Locus of Control on
Cheating: Determinants of the "Congruence Effect". *Journal of
Personality* 46: 72-95.

Katkovsky, Walter, Virginia C. Crandall, and Suzanne Good. 1967.
Parental Antecedents of Children's Beliefs in Internal-External
Control of Reinforcement in Intellectual Achievement Situations.
Child Development 28:765-776.

Kelley, Thomas M. 1996. At-Risk Youth and Locus of Control: Do
They Really See A Choice? *Juvenile & Family Court Journal* 47:39-
53.

Kilpatrick, Dean G., William R. Dubin, and David B. Marcotte. 1974.
Personality, Stress and the Medication Education Process, and
Changes in Affective Mood State. *Psychological Reports* 34:1215-
1223.

Kirk, David S. 2008. The Neighborhood Context of Racial and Ethnic
Disparities in Arrest. *Demography* 45:55-77.

Kirk, David S. 2009. Unraveling the Contextual Effects on Student Suspension and Juvenile Arrest: An Examination of School, Neighborhood, and Family Controls. *Criminology* 47:479-520.

Klebanov, Pamela K., Jeanne Brooks-Gunn, P. Lindsay Chase-Lansdale, and Rachel A. Gordon. 1997. Are Neighborhood Effects on Young Children Mediated by Features of the Home Environment? Pp. 119-144 in *Neighborhood Poverty: Context and Consequences for Children, Volume 1.* eds. Jeanne Brooks-Gunn, Greg J. Duncan, and J. Lawrence Aber. New York: Russell Sage Foundation.

Kornhauser, Ruth. 1978. *Social Sources of Delinquency.* Chicago, IL: University of Chicago Press.

Krause, Neal, and Sheldon Stryker. 1984. Stress and Well-Being: The Buffering Role of Locus of Control Beliefs. *Social Science and Medicine* 18:783-790.

Kreft, Ita G.G., Jan de Leeuw, and Leona S. Aiken. 1995. The Effect of Different Forms of Centering in Hierarchical Linear Models. *Multivariate Behavioral Research* 30:1-21.

Krohn, Marvin D., Terence P. Thornberry, Chris L. Gibson, and Julie M. Baldwin. 2010. The Development and Impact of Self-Report Measures of Crime and Delinquency. *Journal of Quantitative Criminology* 26:509-525.

Kupersmidt, Janis B., Pamela C. Griesler, Melissa E. DeRosier, Charlotte J. Patterson, and Paul W. Davis. 1995. Childhood Aggression and Peer Relations in the Context of Family and Neighborhood Factors. *Child Development* 66:360-375.

Langdon, Peter E., and Tiffany J. Talbot. 2006. Locus of Control and Sex Offenders with an Intellectual Disability. *International Journal of Offender and Comparative Criminology* 50:391-401.

Larson, Reed. 1989. Is Feeling "In Control" Related to Happiness in Daily Life? *Psychological Reports* 64:775-784.

Lau, S., and Kwok Leung. 1992. Self-Concept, Delinquency, Relations with Parents and School and Chinese Adolescents' Perception of Personal Control. *Personality and Individual Differences* 13:615-622.

Laub, John H., and Robert J. Sampson. 2003. *Shared Beginnings, Divergent Lives: Delinquent Boys to Age 70.* Cambridge, MA: Harvard University Press.

Lauritsen, Janet L. 1998. The Age-Crime Debate: Assessing the Limits of Longitudinal Self-Report Data. *Social Forces* 77:127-155.

LeBlanc, Richard F., and Alexander Tolor. 1972. Alienation, Distancing, Externalizing, and Sensation Seeking in Prison Inmates. *Journal of Consulting and Clinical Psychology* 39:514.

Lederer, Jeffrey M., Gary Kielhofner, and Janet Hawkins Watts. 1985. Values, Personal Causation and Skills of Delinquents and Nondelinquents. *Occupational Therapy in Mental Health* 5:59-77.

Lefcourt, Herbert M. 1976. *Locus of Control. Current Trends in Theory and Research.* Hillsdale, NJ: Lawrence-Erlbaum Associates, Inc.

Lefcourt, Herbert M. 1982. *Locus of Control: Current Trends in Theory and Research.* 2nd edition. Hillsdale, NJ: Lawrence-Erlbaum Associates, Inc.

Lefcourt, Herbert M., and Gordon W. Ladwig. 1966. The American Negro: A Problem in Expectancies. *Journal of Personality and Social Psychology* 1:377-380.

Levenson, Hanna. 1975. Multidimensional Locus of Control in Prison Inmates. *Journal of Applied Social Psychology* 5:342-347.

Leventhal, Tama, and Jeanne Brooks-Gunn. 2000. The Neighborhoods They Live In: The Effects of Neighborhood Residence on Child and Adolescent Outcomes. *Psychological Bulletin* 126:309-337.

Lewin, Kurt. 1935. *A Dynamic Theory of Personality.* New York: McGraw-Hill.

Loeber, Rolf, Stephanie M. Green, Kate Keenan, and Benjamin B. Lahey. 1995. Which Boys Will Fare Worse? Early Predictors of the Onset of Conduct Disorder in a Six-Year Longitudinal Study. *Journal of the American Academy of Child and Adolescent Psychiatry* 34:499-509.

Loeber, Rolf, and Magda Stouthamer-Loeber. 1986. Family Factors as Correlates and Predictors of Juvenile Conduct Problems and Delinquency. *Crime and Justice* 7:29-149.

Long, J. Scott, and Jeremy Freese. 2006. *Regression Models for Categorical Dependent Variables Using Stata.* College Station, TX: Stata Press.

Ludwig, Kristin B., and Joe F. Pittman. 1999. Adolescent Prosocial Values and Self-Efficacy in Relation to Delinquency, Risky Sexual Behavior, and Drug Use. *Youth & Society* 30:461-482.

Luke, Douglas A. 2004. *Multilevel Modeling.* Thousand Oaks, CA: Sage.

Lyman, Donald R., Avshalom Caspi, Terrie E. Moffitt, Per-Olof H. Wikström, Rolf Loeber, and Scott Novak. 2000. The Interaction Between Impulsivity and Neighborhood Context on Offending: The Effects of Impulsivity are Stronger in Poorer Neighborhoods. *Journal of Abnormal Psychology* 109:563-574.

Lynch, Shirley, David P. Hurford, and AmyKay Cole. 2002. Parental Enabling Attitudes and Locus of Control of At-Risk and Honors Students. *Adolescence* 37:527-549.

Mack, Kristin Y., Michael J. Leiber, Richard A. Featherstone, and Maria A. Monserud. 2007. Reassessing the Family-Delinquency Association: Do Family Type, Family Processes, and Economic Factors Make a Difference? *Journal of Criminal Justice* 35:51-67.

MacKenzie, Doris Layton, Lynne I. Goodstein, and David C. Blouin. 1987. Personal Control and Prisoner Adjustment: An Empirical Test of a Proposed Model. *Journal of Research in Crime and Delinquency* 24:496-68.

Maimon, David, and Christopher R. Browning. 2010. Unstructured Socializing, Collective Efficacy, and Violent Behavior Among Urban Youth. *Criminology* 48:443-474.

Marsa, Fiona, Gary O'Reilly, Alan Carr, Paul Murphy, Maura O'Sullivan, Anthony Cotter, and David Hevey. 2004. Attachment Styles and Psychological Profiles of Child Sex Offenders in Ireland. *Journal of Interpersonal Violence* 19:228-251.

Matherene, Monique M., and Adrian Thomas. 2001. Family Environment as a Predictor of Adolescent Delinquency. *Adolescence* 36:655-664.

Maxwell, Christopher D., Joel H. Garner, and Wesley G. Skogan. 2011. *Collective Efficacy and Criminal Behavior in Chicago, 1995-2004.* Washington, DC: U.S. Department of Justice.

Mayer, Susan E., and Christopher Jencks. 1989. Growing Up in Poor Neighborhoods: How Much Does It Matter? *Science* 243:1441-1445.

McLeod, Jane D., Candace Kruttschnitt, and Maude Dornfeld. 1994. Does Parenting Explain the Effects of Structural Conditions on Children's Antisocial Behavior? A Comparison of Blacks and Whites. *Social Forces* 73:575-604.

Miethe, Terance D., Jodi Olson, and Ojmarrh Mitchell. 2006. Specialization and Persistence in the Arrest Histories of Sex Offenders: A Comparative Analysis of Alternative Measures and Offense Types. *Journal of Research in Crime and Delinquency* 43:204-229.

Miller, Christi Allen, Trey Fitch, and Jennifer L. Marshall. 2003. Locus of Control and At-Risk Youth: A Comparison of Regular Education High School Students and Students in Alternative Schools. *Education* 123:548-551.

Mirowsky, John, and Catherine E. Ross. 1990. Control or Defense? Depression and the Sense of Control Over Good and Bad Outcomes. *Journal of Health and Social Behavior* 31:71-86.

Mischel, Walter, Robert Zeiss, and Antonette Zeiss. 1974. An Internal-External Control Test for Young Children. *Journal of Personality and Social Psychology* 29:265-278.

Moffitt, Terrie E., Avshalom Caspi, Michael Rutter, and Phil A. Silva. 2001. *Sex Differences in Antisocial Behavior: Conduct Disorder, Delinquency, and Violence in the Dunedin Longitudinal Study.* Cambridge, UK: Cambridge University Press.

Molnar, Beth E., Magdalena Cerda, Andrea L. Roberts, and Stephen L. Buka. 2008. Effects of Neighborhood Resources on Aggressive and Delinquent Behaviors Among Urban Youths. *American Journal of Public Health* 98:1086-1093.

Molnar, Beth E., Matthew J. Miller, Deborah Azrael, and Stephen L. Buka. 2004. Neighborhood Predictors of Concealed Firearm Carrying among Children and Adolescents: Results from the Project on Human Development in Chicago Neighborhoods. *Archives of Pediatrics and Adolescent Medicine* 158:657-664.

Moos, Rudolf H., and Charles J. Holahan. 2003. Dispositional and Contextual Perspectives on Coping: Toward an Integrative Framework. *Journal of Clinical Psychology* 59:1387-1403.

Morelli, George, Herb Krotinger, and Sharon Moore. 1979. Neuroticism and Levenson's Locus of Control Scale. *Psychological Reports* 44:153-154.

Morenoff, Jeffrey D. 2003. Neighborhood Mechanisms and the Spatial Dynamics of Birth Weight. *American Journal of Sociology* 108:976-1017.

Mosher, Clayton J., Terance D. Miethe, and Dretha M. Phillips. 2002. *The Mismeasure of Crime.* Thousand Oaks, CA: Sage.

Nagin, Daniel S. 2007. Moving Choice to Center Stage in Criminological Research and Theory - The American Society of Criminology 2006 Sutherland Address. *Criminology* 45:259-272.

Nagin, Daniel S., and Raymond Paternoster. 1991. On the Relationship of Past to Future Participation in Delinquency. *Criminology* 29:163-189.

Nowicki, Stephen, and Julia Roundtree. 1971. Correlates of Locus of Control in a Secondary School Population. *Developmental Psychology* 4:477-478.

Nowicki, Stephen, and Bonnie R. Strickland. 1973. A Locus of Control Scale for Children. *Journal of Consulting and Clinical Psychology* 40:148-154.

Obitz, Frederick W., L. Jerome Oziel, and John J. Unmacht. 1973. General and Specific Perceived Locus of Control in Delinquent Drug Users. *The International Journal of the Addictions* 8:723-727.

Olds, David L., John Eckenrode, Charles R. Henderson, Jr., Harriet Kitzman, Jane Powers, Robert Cole, Kimberly Sidora, Pamela Morris, Lisa M. Pettitt, and Dennis Luckey. 1997. Long-Term Effects of Home Visitation on Maternal Life Course and Child Abuse and Neglect. *Journal of the American Medical Association* 278:637-643.

Olds, David L., Charles R. Henderson, Jr., Robert Cole, John Eckenrode, Harriet Kitzman, Dennis Luckey, Lisa Pettitt, Kimberly

Sidora, Pamela Morris, and Jane Powers. 1998. Long-Term Effects of Nurse Home Visitation on Children's Criminal and Antisocial Behavior. *Journal of the American Medical Association* 280:1238-1244.

Ollendick, Thomas H., and Michel Hersen. 1979. Social Skills Training for Juvenile Delinquents. *Behavior Research and Therapy* 17:547-554.

Parrott, C.A., and K.T. Strongman. 1984. Locus of Control and Delinquency. *Adolescence* 74: 459-471.

Paternoster, Ray, and Greg Pogarsky. 2009. Rational Choice, Agency and Thoughtfully Reflective Decision Making: The Short and Long-Term Consequences of Making Good Choices. *Journal of Quantitative Criminology* 25:103-127.

Paternoster, Ray, Greg Pogarsky, and Gregory Zimmerman. 2011. Thoughtfully Reflective Decision Making and the Accumulation of Capital: Bringing Choice Back In. *Journal of Quantitative Criminology* 27:1-26.

Pearlin, Leonard I., and Carmi Schooler. 1978. The Structure of Coping. *Journal of Health and Social Behavior* 19:2-21.

Pearlin, Leonard I., Elizabeth G. Menaghan, Morton A. Lieberman, and Joseph T. Mullan. 1981. The Stress Process. *Journal of Health and Social Behavior* 22:337-356.

Peiser, Nadine C., and Patrick C.L. Heaven. 1996. Family Influences on Self-Reported Delinquency Among High School Students. *Journal of Adolescence* 19:557-568.

Phares, E. Jerry. 1976. *Locus of Control in Personality*. Morristown, NJ: General Learning Press.

Piquero, Alex, David P. Farrington, Brandon C. Welsh, Richard Tremblay, and Wesley G. Jennings. 2009. Effects of Early Family/Parent Training Programs on Antisocial Behavior and Delinquency. *Journal of Experimental Criminology* 5:83-120.

Piquero, Alex, Raymond Paternoster, Paul Mazerolle, Robert Brame, and Charles W. Dean. 1999. Onset Age and Offense Specialization. *Journal of Research in Crime and Delinquency* 36:275-299.

Porter, Chebon A., and Patricia J. Long. 1999. Locus of Control and Adjustment in Female Adult Survivors of Childhood Sexual Abuse. *Journal of Child Sexual Abuse* 8:3-25.

Pratt, Travis, and Francis T. Cullen. 2000. The Empirical Status of Gottfredson and Hirschi's General Theory of Crime: A Meta-Analysis. *Criminology* 38:931-964.

Pratt, Travis, and Francis T. Cullen. 2005. Assessing Macro-Level Predictors and Theories of Crime: A Meta-Analysis. *Crime and Justice* 32:373-438.

Pugh, David N. 1993. The Effects of Problem-Solving Ability and Locus of Control on Prisoner Adjustment. *International Journal of Offender Therapy and Comparative Criminology* 37:163-176.

Raubenheimer, J. 2004. An Item Selection Procedure to Maximize Scale Reliability and Validity. *South African Journal of Industrial Psychology* 30:59-64.

Raudenbush, Stephen W., and Anthony S. Bryk. 2002. *Hierarchical Linear Models. Applications and Data Analysis Methods.* Thousand Oaks, CA: Sage.

Reiss, Albert J. 1986. Why are Communities Important in Understanding Crime? Pp. 1-33 in *Communities and Crime*. eds. Albert J. Reiss and Michael H. Tonry. Chicago, IL: Chicago University Press.

Reitzel, Lorraine R., and Beverly Harju. 2000. Influence of Locus of Control and Custody Level on Intake and Prison-Adjustment Depression. *Criminal Justice and Behavior* 27:625-644.

Reynolds, Carl H. 1976. Correlational Findings, Educational Implications, and Criticisms of Locus of Control Research. *Journal of Black Studies* 6:221-256.

Ross, Catherine E., John R. Reynolds, and Karlyn J. Geis. 2000. The Contingent Meaning of Neighborhood Stability for Residents' Psychological Well-Being. *American Sociological Review* 65:581-597.

Rotter, Julian B. 1954. *Social Learning and Clinical Psychology.* Englewood Cliffs, NJ: Prentice Hall.

Rotter, Julian B. 1966. Generalized Expectancies for Internal Versus External Control of Reinforcement. *Psychological Monographs* 80 (Whole No. 609).

Rotter, Julian B. 1990. Internal Versus External Control of Reinforcement: A Case History of a Variable. *American Psychologist* 45:489-493.

Sampson, Robert J. 1987. Urban Black Violence: The Effect of Male Joblessness and Family Disruption. *American Journal of Sociology* 93:348-382.

Sampson, Robert J. 1992. Family Management and Child Development: Insights from Social Disorganization Theory. Pp. 63-93 in *Facts, Frameworks, and Forecasts, Advances in Criminological Theory, Volume 3.* ed. Joan McCord. New Brunswick, NJ: Transaction.

Sampson, Robert J. 2006. How Does Community Context Matter? Social Mechanisms and the Explanation of Crime Rates. Pp. 31-60 in *The Explanation of Crime.* eds. Per-Olof H. Wikström and Robert J. Sampson. Cambridge, UK: Cambridge University.

Sampson, Robert J., and Dawn J. Bartusch. 1998. Legal Cynicism and (Subcultural?) Tolerance of Deviance: The Neighborhood Context of Racial Differences. *Law & Society Review* 32:777-804.

Sampson, Robert J., and W. Byron Groves. 1989. Community Structure and Crime: Testing Social-Disorganization Theory. *American Journal of Sociology* 94:774-802.

Sampson, Robert J., and John H. Laub. 1993. *Crime in the Making: Pathways and Turning Points Through Life.* Cambridge, MA: Harvard University Press.

Sampson, Robert J., and John H. Laub. 1995. Understanding Variability in Lives Through Time: Contributions of Life-Course Criminology. *Studies on Crime & Crime Prevention* 4:143-158.

Sampson, Robert J., and Jeffrey D. Morenoff. 1997. Ecological Perspectives on the Neighborhood Context of Urban Poverty: Past and Present. Pp. 1-22 in *Neighborhood Poverty: Policy Implications in Studying Neighborhoods, Volume 2.* eds. Jeanne Brooks-Gunn, Greg J. Duncan, and J. Lawrence Aber. New York: Russell Sage Foundation.

Sampson, Robert J., Jeffrey D. Morenoff, and Thomas Gannon-Rowley. 2002. Assessing "Neighborhood Effects": Social Processes and New Directions in Research. *Annual Review of Sociology* 28:443-478.

Sampson, Robert J., Jeffrey D. Morenoff, and Stephen Raudenbush. 2005. Social Anatomy of Racial and Ethnic Disparities in Violence. *American Journal of Public Health* 95:224-232.

Sampson, Robert J., and Stephen W. Raudenbush. 1999. Systematic Social Observation of Public Spaces: A New Look at Disorder in Urban Neighborhoods. *American Journal of Sociology* 105:603-651.

Sampson, Robert J., Stephen W. Raudenbush, and Felton Earls. 1997. Neighborhoods and Violent Crime: A Multilevel Study of Collective Efficacy. *Science* 277:918-924.

Sampson, Robert J., and Patrick Sharkey. 2008. Neighborhood Selection and the Social Reproduction of Concentrated Racial Inequality. *Demography* 45:1-29.

Sampson, Robert J., and William Julius Wilson. 1995. Toward a Theory of Race, Crime, and Urban Inequality. Pp. 37-54 in Crime and Inequality. eds. John Hagan and Ruth Peterson. Stanford, CA: Stanford University Press.

Sandler, Irwin N., and Brian Lakey. 1982. Locus of Control as a Stress Moderator: The Role of Control Perception and Social Support. *American Journal of Community Psychology* 10:65-80.

Scales, Peter C. 1999. Reducing Risks and Building Developmental Assets: Essential Actions for Promoting Adolescent Health. *Journal of School Health* 69:113-119.

Scholz, Urte, Benicio Gutiérrez Doña, Shonali Sud, and Ralf Schwarzer. 2002. Is General Self-Efficacy a Universal Construct? Psychometric Findings from 25 Countries. *European Journal of Psychological Assessment* 18:242-251.

Schreck, Christopher J., Jean Marie McGloin, and David S. Kirk. 2009. On the Origins of the Violent Neighborhood: A Study of the Nature and Predictors of Crime-Type Differentiation across Chicago Neighborhoods. *Justice Quarterly* 26:771-794.

Schwarzer, Ralf, and Aristi Born. 1997. Optimistic Self-Beliefs: Assessment of General Perceived Self-Efficacy in Thirteen Cultures. *World Psychology* 3:177-190.

Scott, Jacqueline, and Duane Alwin. 1998. Retrospective versus Prospective Measurement of Life Histories in Longitudinal Research. Pp. 98-127 in *Methods of Life Course Research: Qualitative and Quantitative Approaches*. eds. Janet Z. Giele and Glen H. Elder, Jr. Thousand Oaks, CA: Sage.

Seligman, Martin E. P. 1975. *Helplessness: On Depression, Development, and Death.* San Francisco, CA: Freeman.

Sharkey, Patrick T. 2006. Navigating Dangerous Streets: The Sources and Consequences of Street Efficacy. *American Sociological Review* 71:826-846.

Sharkey, Patrick T., and Robert J. Sampson. 2010. Destination Effects: Residential Mobility and Trajectories of Adolescent Violence in a Stratified Metropolis. *Criminology* 48: 639-681.

Shaw, Clifford R., and Henry D. McKay 1942/1969. *Juvenile Delinquency and Urban Areas*. Chicago, IL: University of Chicago Press.

Silbereisen, Rainer K., and Klaus Eyferth. 1986. Development as Action in Context. Pp. 3-16 in *Development as Action in Context.* eds. Rainer K. Silbereisen, Klaus Eyferth, and Georg Rudinger. New York: Springer-Verlag.

Silver, Eric, and Lisa L. Miller. 2004. Sources of Informal Social Control in Chicago Neighborhoods. *Criminology* 42:551-583.

Simons, Ronald L., Leslie Gordon Simons, Callie Harbin Burt, Gene H. Brody, and Carolyn Curtrona. 2005. Collective Efficacy, Authoritative Parenting and Delinquency: A Longitudinal Test of a Model Integrating Community- and Family-Level Processes. *Criminology* 43:989-1029.

Smith, Douglas A., and G. Roger Jarjoura. 1988. Social Structure and Criminal Victimization. *Journal of Research in Crime and Delinquency* 25:27-52.

Smith, Douglas A., and Christy A. Visher. 1980. Sex and Involvement in Deviance/Crime: A Quantitative Review of the Empirical Literature. *American Sociological Review* 65:767-782.

Snijders, Tom A.B., and Roel J. Bosker. 1999. *Multilevel Analysis: An Introduction to Basic and Multilevel Modeling.* Thousand Oaks, CA: Sage.

Steenbeek, Wouter, and John R. Hipp. 2011. A Longitudinal Test of Social Disorganization Theory: Feedback Effects Among Cohesion, Social Control, and Disorder. *Criminology* 49:833-871.

Steffensmeier, Darrell J., and Emilie Allan. 1996. Gender and Crime: Toward a Gendered Theory of Female Offending. *Annual Review of Sociology* 22:459-487.

Steffensmeier, Darrell J., Jennifer Schwartz, Hua Zhong, and Jeff Ackerman. 2005. An Assessment of Recent Trends in Girls' Violence using Diverse Longitudinal Sources: Is the Gender Gap Closing? *Criminology* 43:355-406.

Sutherland, Edwin. 1947. *Principles of Criminology.* 4th edition. Philadelphia, PA: Lippincott.

Taylor, Ralph B. 2010. Communities, Crime, and Reactions to Crime Multilevel Models: Accomplishments and Meta-Challenges. *Journal of Quantitative Criminology* 26:455-466.

Thomas, William I., and Florian W. Znaniecki. 1918-1920. *The Polish Peasant in Europe and America: Monograph of an Immigrant.* Boston, MA: Gorham Press.

Thompson, Martie P., and Fran H. Norris. 1992. Crime, Social Status, and Alienation. *American Journal of Community Psychology* 20:97-119.

Thornberry, Terence P., and Marvin D. Krohn. 2000. The Self-Report Method for Measuring Delinquency and Crime. Pp. 33-83 in *Measurement and Analysis of Crime and Justice, Criminal Justice 2000, Volume 4.* ed. David Duffee. Washington, DC: U.S. Department of Justice.

Tipton, Robert M., and Everett L. Worthington, Jr. 1984. The Measurement of Generalized Self-Efficacy: A Study of Construct Validity. *Journal of Personality Assessment* 48:545-548.

Tonry, Michael, Lloyd E. Ohlin, and David P. Farrington. 1991. *Human Development and Criminal Behavior.* New York: Springer-Verlag.

Twenge, Jean M., Linqin Zhang, and Charles Im. 2004. It's Beyond My Control: A Cross-Temporal Meta-Analysis of Increasing Externality in Locus of Control, 1960-2002. *Personality and Social Psychology Review* 8:308-319.

Van Gelder, Jean-Louis, and Reinout E. De Vries. 2012. Traits and States: Integrating Personality and Affect into a Model of Criminal Decision Making. *Criminology.*

Van Voorhis, Patricia, Francis T. Cullen, Richard A. Mathers, and Connie Chenoweth Garner. 1988. The Impact of Family Structure and Quality on Delinquency: A Comparative Assessment of Structural and Functional Factors. *Criminology* 26:235-261.

Warner, Barbara D., and Keri Burchfield. 2011. Misperceived Neighborhood Values and Informal Social Control. *Justice Quarterly* 28:606-630.

Warr, Mark. 2002. *Companions in Crime: The Social Aspects of Criminal Conduct.* Cambridge, UK: Cambridge University Press.

Weisburd, David. 2012. Bringing Social Context Back Into the Equation. The Importance of Social Characteristics of Places in the Prevention of Crime. *Criminology & Public Policy* 11:317-326.

Wells, L. Edward, and Joseph H. Rankin. 1991. Families and Delinquency: A Meta-Analysis of the Impact of Broken Homes. *Social Problems* 38:71-93.

West, Donald J., and David P. Farrington. 1973. *Who Becomes Delinquent?* London: Heinemann.

Wheaton, Blair. 1983. Stress, Personal Coping Resources, and Psychiatric Symptoms. *Journal of Health and Social Behavior* 27:78-89.

Wheaton, Blair, and Philippa Clarke. 2003. Space Meets Time: Integrating Temporal and Contextual Influences on Mental Health in Early Adulthood. *American Sociological Review* 68:680-706.

Wikström, Per-Olof H. 2004. Crime as Alternative: Towards a Cross-Level Situational Action Theory of Crime Causation. Pp. 1-37 in *Institutions and Intentions in the Study of Crime: Beyond Empiricism, Advances in Criminological Theory, Volume 13.* ed. Joan McCord. New Brunswick, NJ: Transaction.

Wikström, Per-Olof H. 2006. Individuals, Settings, and Acts of Crime: Situational Mechanisms and the Explanation of Crime. Pp. 61-107 in *The Explanation of Crime*. eds. Per-Olof H. Wikström and Robert J. Sampson. Cambridge, UK: Cambridge University.

Wikström, Per-Olof H., and Rolf Loeber. 2000. Do Disadvantaged Neighborhoods Cause Well-Adjusted Children to Become Adolescent Delinquents? A Study of Male Juvenile Serious Offending, Individual Risk and Protective Factors, and Neighborhood Context. *Criminology* 38:1109-1142.

Wikström, Per-Olof H., and Robert J. Sampson. 2003. Social Mechanisms of Community Influences on Crime and Pathways in Criminality. Pp. 118-148 in *Causes of Conduct Disorder and Juvenile Delinquency*. eds. Benjamin B. Lahey, Terrie E. Moffitt, and Avshalom Caspi. New York: Guilford Press.

Wilson, James Q., and Richard J. Herrnstein. 1985. *Crime and Human Nature*. New York: Simon and Schuster.

Wilson, William Julius. 1987. *The Truly Disadvantaged: The Inner City, the Underclass, and Public Policy*. Chicago, IL: University of Chicago Press.

Wilson, William Julius. 1991. Studying Inner-City Social Dislocations: The Challenge of Public Agenda Research. 1990 Presidential Address. *American Sociological Review* 56:1-14.

Wolfgang, Marvin, Terence Thornberry, and Robert Figlio. 1987. *From Boy to Man: From Delinquency to Crime*. Chicago, IL: University of Chicago Press.

Zimmerman, Gregory M., and Steven F. Messner. 2011. Neighborhood Context and Nonlinear Peer Effects on Adolescent Violent Crime. *Criminology* 49:873-903

Index

0 1341 1573063 9

DATE DUE	RETURNED